Britain's Plot to Kill Hitler

Britain's Plot to Kill Hitler

The True Story of Operation Foxley and SOE

Eric Lee

Foreword by Ian Kershaw

Greenhill Books

Britain's Plot to Kill Hitler:
The True Story of Operation Foxley and SOE

Greenhill Books

First published by Greenhill Books, 2022
Greenhill Books, c/o Pen & Sword Books Ltd,
47 Church Street, Barnsley, S. Yorkshire, S70 2AS
For more information on our books, please visit
www.greenhillbooks.com, email contact@greenhillbooks.com
or write to us at the above address.

Copyright © Eric Lee, 2022

All rights reserved. No part of this publication may be reproduced, stored in or introduced into a retrieval system, or transmitted, in any form, or by any means (electronic, mechanical, photocopying, recording or otherwise) without the prior written permission of the publisher. Any person who does any unauthorised act in relation to this publication may be liable to criminal prosecution and civil claims for damages.

CIP data records for this title are available from the British Library
ISBN 978-1-78438-727-3

Typeset by JCS Publishing Services Ltd
Typeset in 12/15pt Minion Pro
Printed and bound in Great Britain by
CPI Group (UK) Ltd, Croydon, CR0 4YY

Contents

Foreword by Ian Kershaw — vii

1. "We Are Not Mad, Nor Is This a Joke" — 1
2. Man Hunt — 8
3. The Unlikely Assassin — 14
4. The Perfect Murder — 19
5. The Manchurian Candidate — 26
6. "Peace on Earth to All Men of Good Will" — 38
7. Combined Operation — 41
8. Stalin's "Hitler Scheme" — 44
9. "Professor Moriarty" — 52
   Conclusion — 58

Appendix: HS 6/624: "Operation FOXLEY" — 65

Notes — 189
Bibliography — 197
Acknowledgements — 201

Foreword

It should probably have been no surprise that secret plans to assassinate Hitler (and a number of subordinate Nazi leaders) were mooted in Britain during the war. But it certainly *was* a surprise when the news of Operation Foxley broke. The sensation in the press showed how closely the secret had been guarded. There was surprise, too, at the extent and quality of SOE's intelligence on Hitler's surroundings and movements at his Alpine retreat near Berchtesgaden, in southern Bavaria, and on his security arrangements. Some of this new information makes a notable addition to previous knowledge. The publication of the full dossier on Foxley is, therefore, greatly to be welcomed, above all for the intriguing insight it provides into thinking in top British intelligence circles during the last phase of the war and the possible methods of carrying out the assassination.

Among the most revealing papers in the files, in my view, are the conflicting assessments of the desirability of killing Hitler. SOE's senior staff officers were sharply divided in their views. The argument that killing Hitler would ensure his martyrdom in the eyes of the German population, and that his bungling war strategy (as SOE chiefs saw it) made him worth more alive than dead to the Allies, was countered by the view that the German war effort would collapse almost overnight if Hitler were eliminated. The varying responses of historians and other commentators to the papers on their release showed that widely differing interpretations still prevail more than half a century later.

How desirable it would have been to assassinate Hitler depends in some measure on the timing. According to one memorandum in the dossier, SOE had considered such a move in 1941, only – for reasons not disclosed – to discard the proposition. The killing of Hitler at that date – though it is, in fact, doubtful in the extreme that it could have been accomplished – would have had seismic consequences for the course of the war. By late June 1944, when Foxley was seriously discussed for the first time, that was less clear. The Allied landing in Normandy had by then been successfully consolidated, though the advance was still slow and German resistance tenacious. In the East, the Red Army was making notable advances, even if a mighty struggle, ending in the streets of Berlin, still lay ahead. The war was far from over. But the days of the Hitler regime were plainly numbered. Allied strategy had long been targeted at the *total* defeat of Germany, embodied in the policy of "unconditional surrender" proclaimed at the Casablanca Conference in January 1943. This aim was now in sight.

Of course, a successful assassination of Hitler *might* have helped realize that aim earlier than it was in fact attained, and *might* have brought a more rapid end to the war. This would have spared much of the immense human misery and suffering which mounted drastically in the last months of the conflagration. The victims of the unbelievable inhumanity in the concentration camps would have been released from their torture much earlier. Many who succumbed in the last months would have lived. In Germany itself, the carnage in Dresden and other cities obliterated by Allied bombing in the final phase of the war would not have taken place. And the continuing enormous military losses on the eastern and western fronts, including those resulting from the last great German offensive in the Ardennes, the "Battle of the Bulge", initiated directly by

Foreword

Hitler, would have been avoided. The *potential* gains from an assassination of Hitler were, therefore, massive. Even without the advantage of hindsight into the magnitude of what might have been achieved, it is easy to see why some of the SOE chiefs were drawn to Operation Foxley.

But it is also possible that the killing of Hitler would not have accelerated the end of the war. Most probably, as other SOE strategists argued, a successful assassination by enemy forces (and, as was pointed out, this would inevitably have been recognised) would have brought an intense rallying round the cult of the "martyred" Führer and a strengthening of the fanaticised minority of the population which remained, despite all setbacks, fervent and devoted believers in Hitler. Many of these had burnt their boats in the genocidal policies of the regime and would have been unlikely to throw away their arms unless some self-serving deal could have been struck with the Western Allies. Göring or, more probably, Himmler would most likely have taken over as the next leader. It is doubtful that power would have passed to the Wehrmacht. Most of the leading oppositional figures in the army had in any case been arrested, many of them killed, following the ill-fated Stauffenberg attempt on Hitler's life on 20 July 1944 (which had brought a big upsurge in support for the Führer). Many of the remaining generals were either Hitler loyalists or politically supine. The most likely guess is that the war would have continued, at least for the time being, while the next leader tried to negotiate a peace separating the Western Allies from the Soviet Union – something the Nazi leadership had always strived for. If the Western Allies entertained such a separate peace – which would have been highly unlikely, and would have flown in the face of the "unconditional surrender" policy with victory practically there for the taking – the breach with the Soviet Union would have come before it actually did; before, that is, a total defeat of Germany had been achieved. This would scarcely have altered the postwar balance of power in eastern Europe. But it might well have enhanced the prospect of more than just a "Cold War" between

East and West in the following years. Without such a separate peace, however – without, that is, negotiated terms leaving the Allies with less than the unconditional surrender they sought – it is not easy to see why the Germans, even without Hitler, would have seen an alternative to fighting on to the bitter end.

When that end inevitably did come, the task of rebuilding a democratic Germany would have been made immeasurably more difficult by a successful assassination of Hitler. As those SOE chiefs who opposed Foxley claimed, a new version of the stab-in-the-back legend that had poisoned politics in the Weimar Republic and shored up the myth that the German forces had not been militarily defeated would have persisted. As it was, according to public opinion surveys, a quarter of those asked in West Germany in 1952 still thought well of Hitler, and a third opposed the attack on his life by the German Resistance in 1944. It takes little to imagine how easily, in the event of the SOE assassination plan proving successful, defeat could have been blamed within Germany on a cowardly assassination of the heroic Führer by enemy agents. Rebuilding Germany would have been all the harder with that allegation still lingering.

Actually, there was no question of a final decision having to be taken on whether to go ahead with Foxley. By the time the assassination plan had been fully devised, in spring 1945, the end of the war was imminent. Foxley, as SOE realised, had been overtaken by events. The point of any hazardous assassination attempt was by now even more dubious than it had been at the inception of the plan. In fact, the timing and character of the feasibility studies of Foxley meant that the plan in any case never had a chance of being put into operation. All the designs for an assassination attempt were predicated on the attack taking place either at Hitler's residence at the Berghof – the huge complex surrounding his Alpine residence on the Obersalzberg, above Berchtesgaden – or on his special train, while it was stationed in that area or travelling from that region. The meeting to instigate Foxley took place on 28 June 1944. The plans were still under

Foreword

deliberation in early 1945. But Hitler had left the Berghof on 14 July 1944, never to return there. Scarcely two weeks existed, therefore, between the decision to put together a plan to kill Hitler and the last moment when that plan could have been executed. Foxley, it must be concluded, was defunct even before an operational plan could be put together.

Ian Kershaw

— 1 —

"We Are Not Mad, Nor Is This a Joke"

The story of Operation Foxley, the secret British plan to kill the German Führer Adolf Hitler, began with what would today be called a bit of "fake news".

On 19 June 1944, a telegram reached London from an agent of the Special Operations Executive (SOE) in Algiers.[1] The SOE, set up by British Prime Minister Winston Churchill in the early days of the Second World War, was tasked with "setting Europe ablaze". Its agents were scattered all over the territories controlled by the Axis powers and were busy gathering intelligence and stirring up trouble wherever they could.

The SOE agent claimed that a "reliable source", in this case a French colonel, had reported that Hitler was hiding in a chateau in Perpignan, in south-west France. If true, it presented an opportunity to kill him. It was suggested that the chateau be bombed.[2]

The message ended with these words: "WE ARE NOT REPEAT NOT MAD NOR IS THIS A JOKE."

As it turned out, Hitler was not even close to Perpignan.[3] But a day later, a memo drafted by General Hastings Ismay at the War Cabinet – marked "Please destroy after reading" – reminded the chiefs of staff that "in 1941 S.O.E. had a project for eliminating Hitler and that this received the approval of all Departments."[4] He added that circumstances had suddenly changed and "the operation had to be abandoned." No further details were given. Ismay wanted to know if the chiefs had any objection to a resumption of the planning.

Though SOE would not have been involved in a bombing raid, the question of killing the German leader was now on the table, even if the intelligence received from France looked dubious. On 28 June the leading figures in SOE decided to look into the possibility of killing Hitler. They were not unanimous; among others, the head of Section X (Germany), Lieutenant Colonel Ronald H. Thornley, opposed resuming the operation that General Ismay had mentioned. But Air Vice Marshall Ritchie and others wanted to go ahead. Major H.B. Court was put in charge of coming up with a plan. It was to be called Operation Foxley.

Operation Foxley raised a number of questions which SOE needed to address. *Should* it be done? Would killing Hitler shorten the war, or lengthen it? *Could* it be done? Hitler was, after all, the most heavily guarded man on the planet and had survived dozens of assassination attempts.

The idea of assassinating Hitler had come up even before an initial operation was approved in 1941. In fact, there are references going back to 1938, when a British diplomat in Berlin suggested that his residence offered a perfect spot for a sniper to shoot the Führer. In July 1940, an official in the Air Ministry raised the possibility of killing the Nazi leader by the RAF bombing an expected German victory parade in Paris. And in 1941, after the German invasion of the Soviet Union, the British provided intelligence to their new allies indicating where Hitler might be found, in order to allow the Soviet Air Force to launch a raid.

There were many attempts on Hitler's life over the course of a number of years; none of them succeeded. There were at least 46 attempts from 1921 until 1945. There are many reasons why Hitler proved so hard to kill, not least of them being that he was very well guarded, especially after the start of the Second World War.

Following the 28 June meeting, over the course of several months in 1944, SOE officers collated reams of intelligence. In the end they produced a thick dossier laying out several different ways to kill Hitler. That dossier is reproduced in full in the second part of this book.

The plans included shooting him, blowing up his train, poisoning his drinking water, aerial bombardment of his home, and even dropping a parachute battalion on his headquarters. The ideas ranged from a single gunman to an entire battalion of elite troops, and from the eminently practical to the rather crazy. (Although, as we shall see, what may appear crazy now was not necessarily the case at that time.)

While they were busy looking into the technical issues of *how* an assassination of Hitler might be carried out, the SOE leaders were also engaged in a vigorous discussion of *whether* it would be a good idea. In the view of some, the entire Nazi regime rested on the shoulders of this one man, and his death might bring the whole "Thousand Year Reich" crumbling down. Others argued that whatever Hitler's successes as a military strategist early in the war, by 1944 he was a liability to the Germans. His presence at the head of the Third Reich's war machine ensured a swifter end to the fighting.

The legality and ethics of killing Hitler were not seriously addressed at that time. Experts in international law today believe that the targeted killing of Hitler would probably have been legal. In an article for the *Yale Journal of International Law*, Michael N. Schmitt wrote that "Targeting specific individuals *during wartime* [my emphasis] generally was considered valid."[5] Reviewing the long history of discussion among scholars, Schmitt discovered that "treachery" was considered central to the question of whether a killing during wartime was legal. A sniper taking a shot at Hitler was probably legal; bribing a member of the Führer's household to poison him was not.

From 1939 onwards, the German leadership was engaged in an aggressive and illegal war, and the regime was therefore more like a criminal gang than a state. The German Nazi leadership was responsible for both war crimes and crimes against humanity on an unprecedented scale. While the preferred option was to arrest and put on trial the Third Reich's leaders at the end of the war, in some cases killing them when the opportunity arose was an equally good option.

One Nazi leader who was brought to justice without a formal trial was Reinhard Heydrich. Heydrich was the head of the Reichssicherheitshauptamt (Reich Main Security Office), second only to SS head Heinrich Himmler. By 1942, he was serving the Reich as ruler of German-occupied Bohemia and Moravia. Earlier in the year, he was in Berlin where he chaired the infamous Wannsee Conference which mapped out plans for the "Final Solution" – what we now call the Holocaust. He was a prime candidate to stand trial at the end of the war, but the British had no problem with him being killed rather sooner. In the spring of 1942, two Czechoslovak men, Jan Kubiš and Jozef Gabčík, who had been trained and equipped by the SOE, assassinated Heydrich in Prague.

The Americans too had some experience with the deliberate killing of Axis leaders during the war. Admiral Isoroku Yamamoto, commander of the Combined Fleet of the Imperial Japanese Navy, was blamed by the Americans for the surprise attack on Pearl Harbor in 1941. A year after the assassination of Heydrich in Prague, Yamamoto's travel plans were discovered when the Americans cracked the Japanese naval code. The opportunity was seized as the Americans launched a dangerous and highly secret operation to intercept his flight. Yamamoto was killed on Bougainville Island when his transport bomber aircraft was shot down by United States Army Air Forces fighters. The plan to kill Yamamoto was called Operation Vengeance – a code name which did little to conceal the Americans' motive. And the British themselves launched a commando raid in 1941 known as Operation Flipper. It apparently aimed to kill or capture Erwin Rommel, commander of German forces in North Africa. Operation Flipper failed to achieve its objective as Rommel had left the target area several weeks before the raid. The targeted assassination of men like Heydrich, Rommel and Yamamoto showed that, when necessary, the Allies would hunt down enemy leaders and kill them. If Heydrich and Yamamoto deserved their deaths, surely Hitler did as well.

The story of Operation Foxley remained a secret until 1998 when the Public Records Office (now called The National Archives) released the material, publishing a dossier in book form. In re-reading the dossier today, nearly a quarter century after it was first published, and taking into account information that has come to light since, this book will focus on a few aspects of Operation Foxley that seem the most interesting, at least to this writer.

Of all the proposals considered, the most likely option discussed by SOE was to infiltrate a sniper into the forests surrounding Hitler's Alpine retreat near Berchtesgaden. The sniper would have a clear shot at the Führer during his daily unguarded stroll along a path to a teahouse. That plan, documented in considerable detail in the dossier, seems nearly identical to the script of a popular Hollywood film made in 1941, *Man Hunt*, which was in turn based on the best-selling British novel *Rogue Male*.

When considering who might carry out the assassination, SOE took their time, finally naming a British officer, Captain Edmund Bennett, who was apparently fluent in German (though they had plenty of native speakers to choose from). But there is little evidence that he was a sniper. And he was, at the time, thousands of miles away from Europe. As we learned decades after the end of the war, he suffered from astigmatism and was a poor shot. That's odd in itself, but it is hardly the oddest thing one finds in Operation Foxley.

There was considerable thought given to how to poison Hitler and other members of his entourage. A number of possible poisons were considered but these appear only as code names in the documents. There is some evidence that the poison SOE favoured was a relatively obscure one. It became well known only some 15 years after the war when it was central to the plot of an Agatha Christie story, *The Pale Horse*.

One of the ideas that came up relatively early in the process was known as "Foxley II": the targeting of Nazi leaders other than Hitler. One idea was to infiltrate an individual into Germany who might gain access to Himmler and kill him – if he had previously been hypnotised to do so. That plan resembles the plot of the 1959 novel, *The Manchurian Candidate*. Widely dismissed as the least realistic of the various options considered by SOE, there is actually *something* to the idea, though one needs to be ready to go down a rabbit hole for this part of the story.

The very detailed plans one finds in the Operation Foxley dossier make for fascinating reading – not least because they show how *little* was actually known about Hitler and the other Nazi leaders. For example, we now know that Hitler left his Bavarian retreat in July 1944 for the last time, spending the rest of his life in Berlin and at his military headquarters on both the eastern and western fronts. It was while staying at the Wolfsschanze (Wolf's Lair), Hitler's headquarters in East Prussia, that the most serious attempt was made on his life on 20 July 1944. High-ranking German army officers led by Claus von Stauffenberg nearly succeeded in blowing Hitler up with a bomb fitted with one of the SOE's pencil detonators (though SOE itself had no involvement in the attack). The Führer survived the attempt and eventually spent the final months of the war deep underground, in the Führerbunker in Berlin. But this was unknown in London, and the SOE researchers continued to focus on how he might be killed in Berchtesgaden.

In fact, other than a passing reference to the unsuccessful 20 July plot, the Operation Foxley dossier has nothing at all to say about the many other attempts on the life of Hitler. It is not clear how much SOE knew about these as none of them originated from their organisation.

Among other bits of misinformation one finds in the dossier are reports that Himmler was now running Germany (he wasn't) and that the marriage of Hitler's propaganda minister Joseph Goebbels had unravelled, leading Frau Goebbels to flee to Switzerland with the children (which was not the case). They believed that Hitler could no longer speak (he could) and that Eva Braun was Hitler's secretary (she was a bit more than that). That said, the bulk of the information, much of it from debriefings of captured German soldiers who had served with Hitler's entourage, was accurate and detailed. Only later in the war did the Germans realise that men who had served directly with the Führer were a security risk if captured and were kept away from the front lines.

Hitler could almost certainly have been killed in one or more of the ways described in the file. A more detailed exploration of those ideas is the focus of this book.

– 2 –

Man Hunt

The first thing we see is a forest with dense undergrowth, young pine trees, ferns. We hear the sounds of birds chirping. And then we see a single boot print in the dirt, followed by others. A solitary hunter walks silently, a rucksack on his back and a rifle in his arms. He wears a pair of binoculars around his neck.

He crawls to the edge of a crag and raises the binoculars. He then takes out a telescopic sight, which he attaches carefully to his gun and adjusts the range. He rests the rifle on the rucksack, now laid out in front of him, and takes careful aim. Now we can see what he sees through the lens: two men walking on a terrace, initially with their backs to us. The closer one wears a white uniform. The other, wearing a black suit, is unmistakably the German Führer, Adolf Hitler.

The hunter wipes his brow with his right hand. His right index finger then rests on the trigger. The officer in white leaves Hitler, giving him the Nazi salute. Hitler is in the cross-hairs now, the rifle pointing directly at his heart. Hitler walks slowly towards us, resting his hand on a stone bannister, unaware of any danger. The hunter very slowly squeezes the trigger. Instead of a shot, we hear just a quiet click. The chamber was empty. The gun was not loaded.

The hunter silently laughs and waves towards the German dictator, who will survive – this time. He begins to crawl backwards through the brush, but then has a change of heart. He returns to the edge of the crag, this time loading a bullet into the rifle's chamber. Hitler is once again in his cross-hairs. The hunter's right index finger begins to slowly squeeze the trigger.

These are the opening moments of the 1941 film *Man Hunt*, directed by Fritz Lang and starring Walter Pidgeon as the hunter. The film is based on the acclaimed 1939 novel by Geoffrey Household, *Rogue Male*. That scene comes remarkably close to the plan developed by SOE several years later to kill Adolf Hitler. It is almost as if the best minds in British intelligence, when asked to come up with a plan to kill the Nazi leader, drew inspiration from Dudley Nichols' screenplay for a Hollywood film.

Of all the options SOE came up with in Operation Foxley, a lone soldier hiding in the woods, shooting at Hitler while he took his morning stroll, seemed the most likely. It was also similar to how Hitler himself imagined he might be killed – by a lone sniper. "One day a completely harmless man will establish himself in an attic flat along Wilhelmstrasse," Hitler told his first Gestapo chief, Rudolf Diels, in 1933. "He will be taken for a retired schoolmaster. A solid citizen, with horn-rimmed spectacles, poorly shaven, bearded. He will not allow anyone into his modest room. Here he will install a gun, quietly and without undue haste, and with uncanny patience he will aim it at the Reich Chancellery balcony hour after hour, day after day. And then, one day, he will fire!"[1]

Those drafting the SOE plan were surely aware of *Rogue Male* and *Man Hunt*, not least because the book's author, Geoffrey Household, was himself an SOE agent during the war. But there is no evidence that Household was involved in or even aware of the planning for Operation Foxley.

When SOE was trying to find a time and place where Hitler would be vulnerable, interrogations of captured German soldiers who had served with the Führer revealed one striking fact: since mid-March 1944, almost every morning that Hitler was at his Bavarian retreat, he would go for a two-kilometre stroll (about 15–20 minutes) to the *Teehaus* in his compound.

This daily routine flew in the face of what Hitler himself knew about ensuring his security. "The only preventive measure one can take is to live irregularly – to walk, to drive and to travel at irregular times and unexpectedly," he told colleagues.[2]

He would leave his home, the Berghof, between 10:00 and 11:00, and he insisted on walking alone, as it was the only time in the day that he could be by himself with his thoughts. The SS guards who normally accompanied him were ordered to keep their distance. But the guards kept him within sight at all times, though they were sometimes as much as 500 metres away. In the view of the SOE, it was the only time that Hitler completely let his guard down and he was entirely vulnerable.

That morning stroll, unguarded for up to 20 minutes, was the best chance the British were ever going to get to shoot the Führer. It was a golden opportunity, and it is difficult to understand why Hitler ignored his own advice. Perhaps following so many failed assassination attempts over the years, he truly did believe that he was under some kind of divine protection.

The Operation Foxley dossier devotes several pages to discussing how this would be done. But it opens with an important disclaimer:

> In the absence of first-hand information on the OBERSALZBERG since May of this year and in particular since that *attentat* [attack] of July 20th, it is not possible to say whether security and safety measures have been tightened up as of late, or whether extra precautions are being taken at FHQ only.[3]

The dossier goes into some detail on how an agent could learn whether Hitler was in fact in attendance at the Obersalzberg. One indicator was that a large swastika flag would fly in front of the Berghof when he was there. Another clue to Hitler's presence was that one of his special trains could be found in one of the local railway stations, including Berchtesgaden itself. And a particular tavern in Berchtesgaden was also named – because if Hitler was in the area, members of his special bodyguard unit could be found drinking there in the evenings when off-duty. The level of detail accumulated by SOE about Hitler's residence is enormous, but suffers from several errors. For example, the location of Hitler's study is misplaced. British visitors to the Berghof before the war were clearly not consulted, as they would have spotted these problems.

Shooting Hitler on his morning walk seemed to be the best choice, but there were other options named in the dossier. Hitler would sometimes leave his train at the nearby Klessheim castle and might be targeted there. It was also suggested that an agent might be able to approach Hitler's train and throw a suitcase full of explosives under the carriages – which would clearly be a suicide mission and very unlikely to succeed. As the train was guarded on its entire route, and carried anti-aircraft guns and heavily armed troops, it made for a very unpromising target.

The obstacles facing an SOE agent aiming to reach Hitler in Berchtesgaden would have been considerable. First among the problems was how to get an agent anywhere near the area. One possibility was smuggling an agent in via neutral Switzerland, or Austria which was then part of the German Reich. Another possibility was to come in by parachute – something that SOE already had considerably experience with. But even if an agent could get close to Hitler's compound, the problems did not end there.

The main security force protecting Hitler at the Obersalzberg was known as the Reichsicherheitsdienst (RSD, the Reich Security Service), which consisted of about 20 men. Its commander was Brigadeführer Rattenhuber, who was assisted by Haupsturmführer Müller, formerly of the Waffen-SS. The RSD men, who were mostly from Bavaria, usually wore civilian clothes, but sometimes dressed in the uniform of the Waffen-SS. They patrolled the entire complex, usually accompanied by three dogs, each under the command of a *Hundeführer*.

The very detailed maps presented in the Operation Foxley dossier show that an Allied sniper could get close to the perimeter.

Ideally, he'd be able to get within 100–200 metres of the path Hitler would walk on during his morning stroll. The agent could hide in the dense forest, waiting for the right moment, facing a path that Hitler was known to walk every day, alone and unguarded.

The agent would have to come disguised not as a British big game hunter, as in the film, but in German uniform – specifically the uniform of the German army's mountain troops. The dossier contains considerable detail about this uniform, including the cap, collar patches and so on.

The weapon of choice would be a German-made Mauser Karabiner 98 kurz sniper rifle, with a telescopic sight and a magazine full of explosive bullets. The Mauser company continues to make a version of this rifle even today, and boasts on its website that "the Mauser brand has stood as a symbol for the real, successful hunting experience for over 140 years." In advertising the Mauser 98, the company has come up with this rather catchy slogan: "When the top of the food chain needs to be decided, this rifle is your ultimate partner."[4]

The Mauser may not have been the best possible rifle for the job, in part because it produced a large muzzle flash, which would have made finding the gunman easier for Hitler's bodyguards. However, it was good enough and would work within the expected range – and most important, it was a standard weapon of the German army, fitting the agent's cover. The shooter would also need to be a first-class marksman, trained to use this weapon. In addition to the rifle, he'd carry hand grenades to be used in self-defence, as well as a German Luger pistol fitted with a silencer.

SOE also felt that a backup plan was needed in case the sniper missed. A pair of additional agents would be on site as well, stationed near the *Teehaus*. Those men would not necessarily be British, and recruiting Poles, Russians or Czechs was considered. The second team would be armed with a bazooka or a PIAT gun. The PIAT (which stood for "projector, infantry, anti-tank") was a weapon developed by SOE's own researchers.[5] Though not as good as the American bazooka, the PIAT would do the trick if the sniper failed.

SOE historian M.R.D. Foot described the weapon in this way: "At 34 lb 5 oz (15½ kg) it was heavy, but not too heavy to be fired by one prone man from his shoulder; it was a metre long. It was effective up to fifty yards. The hollow charge, though small, had great penetrating power, and a light tank hit by a PIAT rocket was not likely to move again."[6]

But it also had the disadvantage that, unlike the Mauser, it was a British weapon. SOE was going to considerable lengths to conceal their involvement in the assassination, dressing up its agent as a German soldier and giving him a Luger and a Mauser sniper rifle. Using a PIAT to blow up Hitler's car would seem to be very much a last resort.

The dossier described what would happen in the unlikely case that the sniper failed to kill the Führer. The guards would be distracted, looking in the wrong direction while the second team would fire their PIAT at Hitler's car. "The guards would hardly expect a second attack to be made," it declared confidently.

The SOE plan to shoot Hitler in Berchtesgaden is at its core no different from the story written by Geoffrey Household on the eve of the war and later filmed by Fritz Lang. The central problem faced by SOE was not discovering a vulnerability (they had found that), nor deciding on a weapon, nor even planning how to get an agent close enough to Hitler. What was missing from the Operation Foxley dossier was the agent himself – the man whom the British could entrust with the job of shooting Hitler.

— 3 —

The Unlikely Assassin

Selecting the man who would kill Adolf Hitler presented SOE with a problem. The organisation which had been so successful across occupied Europe (and beyond) had almost no footprint in Germany. "It was hardly SOE's fault that its German section did so badly," M.R.D. Foot wrote. "There was no chance of successful guerrilla action in a country in which so large a slice of the public took the opposite side."[1]

Though SOE may not have had a strong presence inside Germany, they had their pick of potential snipers. One good choice would have been Alfgar Hesketh-Prichard.[2] An SOE agent, Hesketh-Prichard was also a crack shot. His father, a top marksman, founded the British Army's school of sniping and authored a book, *Sniping in France*. Alfgar was credited with killing 45 Germans in one day.[3] Though killed in December 1944, there is no evidence that SOE at any time in that year considered him for the job of killing Hitler.

Lieutenant Colonel Nevill Armstrong, Britain's top expert on sniping, described the perfect candidates for that job. "Stalkers, keepers, poachers, prospectors, trappers, out-of-door people, hill and moorland farmers" were put at the top of a list. "It is useless to try to make a sniper out of every man in a battalion."[4]

The Unlikely Assassin

And yet when the time came to propose a candidate to kill Adolf Hitler, the man proposed was seemingly the "everyman" Armstrong cautioned against.

No qualified snipers, nor native German speakers from Section X, appear to have been put forward as candidates for the mission. Instead, the only name ever suggested for the role played by Walter Pidgeon in *Man Hunt*, the lone hunter carrying a rifle with a telescopic sight, was Captain Edmund Bennett, known as Ted to his friends.[5]

Born in Stockport, near Manchester, in 1919, Ted Bennett "must have had exceptional qualities, for the German Directorate examined in depth his candidature for the assassin's assignment," wrote Denis Rigden in his book on Operation Foxley.[6]

Instead of identifying him early on and preparing him for a possible mission, Bennett was first contacted by Section X only in early 1945 – more than six months after the planning for Operation Foxley had begun, and just weeks before Hitler took his own life in the Führerbunker in Berlin.

Section X was by now headed by an old friend of Major General Colin Gubbins, the Director of SOE. Brigadier Gerald Templer had been in charge of the British Expeditionary Force's security back in 1939. Templer found himself back in England in 1944, recovering from what Foot described as a "ludicrous wound": "He had been pressing well forward in a jeep when a lorry in front of him was hit by an enemy shell; a grand piano hurled out of it crushed him."[7]

In early 1945 Templer sent a telegram to the SOE representative in New York regarding Captain Bennett. Bennett was then working in the Military Research Section of the British Defence Attache's staff in Washington, having arrived there just before Christmas, on 23 December 1944. Templer wrote:

1. For your private information we are considering using this man for a high-priority assassination task which would require his lying low in Germany for [a]

considerable period, collecting [the] necessary intelligence to enable him to do [the] job.
2. Before making official application for him [we] would greatly appreciate your advice as to his suitability.
3. Can you possibly give us this without divulging to him [the] real nature of the task we have in mind?[8]

Templer's telegram made no reference to Hitler. It spoke only of a mission that would require a "considerable period" of "lying low" – at a time when the final collapse of the Third Reich was imminent.

The SOE officer in New York was being asked about Bennett's suitability for a mission, without specifying what that mission might be. Fluency in German might be one requirement and being a skilled sniper another – and it was not clear that Bennett was either. Six days later, SOE had their answer from New York:

Have seen subject. ... He, far from being discouraged by my intimidations [sic] of possible toughness of [the] assignment, showed even greater keenness. ... He however wishes to make one stipulation which is that he will not find himself out of a job on completion of [the] assignment or if [the] German war ends before [the] operation takes place, since his present interesting and specialised employment is good for the duration of both wars. ... He would like to get a permanent clandestine job and says [he would] be happy to live in Germany after [the] war.[9]

Meanwhile, a discussion was taking place among senior SOE officers about some physical details regarding the operative who would carry out the attack on Hitler. They were not told Bennett's name. Dr D.M. Newitt, the SOE's Director of Scientific Research, asked whether "the man who is going to carry out this operation" normally wore glasses, or if he did not do so, could he persuaded to wear them. He also asked if the candidate had false teeth or any "physical peculiarity such as wearing a truss or a false limb".

Templer replied that the agent would wear glasses but was "extremely unlikely" to have any of the aforementioned peculiarities:

> On the question of false teeth, he suggested that Colonel Davies (AD/Z) – to whom the minute was addressed – might "pursue the line [with the boffins] as we can give him [the agent] some false teeth even if he does not want them".[10]

Denis Rigden was horrified at this last phrase:

> Although dental health standards in the 1940s were markedly lower than those today, even in those dark wartime days there must have been few robust young would-be secret agents with any false teeth. It therefore seems that Templer was at least briefly toying with the gruesome idea of having some almost certainly healthy teeth extracted for an unspecified operational reason – perhaps to enable poison to be hidden in one or more hollow artificial teeth.[11]

False teeth or not, Bennett seemed ready to do the job. But it was not to be.

On 26 March, Thornley, the former head of Section X, acting on Templer's behalf, telegraphed New York: "1. Under present circumstances do not feel justified in applying for this officer. 2. May revert later."[12] And that was that.

There is much that is strange about this whole aspect of Operation Foxley. One is the fact that it is was still under consideration as late as the final days of March 1945, with the war's end barely a month away. To be fair, though the war would soon be over, no one knew precisely when that would happen. It was probably correct to continue planning for the possibility that Hitler might still need to be killed.

As Roger Moorhouse wrote, Operation Foxley was not a blueprint for an assassination. "For example, it lacked contingency plans for the infiltration and exfiltration of the assassins. It even lacked assassins … it does not appear that SOE was especially energetic in recruiting an agent."[13]

The choice of Ted Bennett – if indeed he was the choice[14] – was a strange one indeed. As we know, he was not a native German speaker; he was probably not a marksman; and he suffered from blurry vision that may have made him a poor shot.

As Bennett's widow Julia said in 1998, he had astigmatism in one eye and was a terrible shot.

> Firing a machine gun, where you don't have to think about it, was one thing, but I can't imagine him being able to assassinate somebody … I knew nothing about it until the newspaper people told me … I was shocked because I would have thought that this was the sort of thing he would have bragged about after the war … He was never in MI5, he was never in the SOE. His real forte was in technical intelligence and he always insisted that he was a backroom boy.

So what made Bennett a candidate for being the marksman who would shoot Adolf Hitler? Mrs Bennett believed the critical factors behind the SOE's choice of her husband may have been "his knowledge of weapons and his fluent command of German, picked up while working in an east German textile firm for two years before the war".[15]

Bennett's military records consist of a single sheet in The National Archives.[16] There is little to indicate why he was applying for "possible S.O.E. employment". According to a documentary film made in 2018, "the 'SA' in his record indicated a familiarity with small arms, which would include rifles, which they suggest may have been the reason why he was chosen." The same record indicated that Bennett was marked "I.O." – for intelligence officer.[17]

Bennett, who died in 1987, never told anyone about Operation Foxley. "Not once in all the years that they were together did he breathe a single hint of his almost-mission to his wife," reported the *Guardian* when the Foxley papers were declassified in 1998.[18]

— 4 —

The Perfect Murder

Crime writer Peter Swanson had been thinking about what constitutes a perfect murder. "It's a phrase that gets tossed around a lot," he wrote, "and my sense is that a perfect murder is when the murder itself is unsolvable, maybe even undetectable. The victim is dead. The murderer has gotten away with it." He noted that such murders are actually quite rare in crime fiction. "There are lots of 'perfect murder' attempts, but most crime fiction is hinged on the notion that a detective will come along to outsmart the criminal."[1]

One of the great writers of crime fiction who looked for ways to create an "unsolvable" and even "undetectable" murder was Agatha Christie. Fifteen years after the end of the Second World War, Christie, then 70 years old, published a short novel, *The Pale Horse*, that told the story of a series of linked murders.

In her novel, Mark Easterbrook, a London-based intellectual, accidentally discovered that a village pub was at the centre of a murder-for-hire conspiracy. The "clients" who paid to have people killed had to be far from the scene of the crimes, to make certain that they could not be seriously considered as suspects. The murders themselves had to be seen to be natural occurrences.

To catch the criminals, Easterbrook colluded with his friend Ginger to set her up as a possible victim. After he placed his "order" for her to be murdered, Ginger fell ill, just like the other victims. No one understood what was causing her illness, but suddenly Easterbrook had an idea. He phoned up a police inspector he knew. He asked the inspector if Ginger's hair was falling out. "Well, as a matter of fact, I believe it is. High fever, I suppose," said the inspector. "Fever my foot," Easterbrook replied. "What Ginger's suffering from, what they've all suffered from, is *thallium poisoning*," he exclaimed.[2]

Christie's use of thallium in this book has been cited as the first reference to the poison in crime fiction. There are stories of people's lives being saved because someone who had read *The Pale Horse* recognised the symptoms of thallium poisoning.[3]

While thallium may not have been widely known to the general public, for the boffins at Porton Down it turned out to be one of the favoured methods to kill the German Führer. Porton Down is located in the Wiltshire countryside not far from Salisbury. Founded in 1916, it has been described as the "oldest chemical warfare research installation in the world".[4] Now known as the Defence Science and Technology Laboratory (DSTL), the facility's public-facing website has little to say about Porton Down's activities during the war and nowhere mentions Operation Foxley, but it does reassure readers that "no aliens, either alive or dead have ever been taken to Porton Down or any other Dstl site."[5]

By 1944, its scientists were working closely with SOE. In case using a sniper to shoot Hitler didn't work out, poisoning him was seen as a kind of Plan B. For this, SOE needed a poison and apparently settled on thallium for reasons which will become apparent. In Operation Foxley, much attention was given to the possibility of getting a poison into the drinking water on the *Führerzug*, Hitler's private train. The report went into some detail about how water was delivered to the train. "Water for drinking and cooking purposes is taken on at station stops en route between rail hydrants, the hose from the hydrant being either connected up from the fresh-water tank on the roof of the dining car … or from water cocks on either side of the coach," it read.[6]

The Perfect Murder

It was never made entirely clear who would deliver the poison to the train, though it was suggested that a number of French women were employed to clean the train and might be available.

The SOE had considerable experience with poisons by this point in the war, including poisons that could be taken by their own agents in case they were captured by the Germans. This may have been behind the questions posed regarding false teeth in the previous chapter.

The main part of the Foxley plan to poison Hitler did not name the poison that would be used. It began with these words: "'I' has been shown as the most suitable medium, since its effect is not immediate like that of 'R' or 'F'. In fact, taken in sufficiently small doses its symptoms may not appear before 6 or 7 days. Under such circumstances there is no antidote."[7]

Not only did the proposed poison have no antidote, but if taken in small doses over the course of a day, it would produce no initial symptoms in the victim. That delayed effect was described by the report's authors as "its chief advantage since it affords the best chance of the intended victim (Hitler) taking the necessary lethal quantity before suspicion has been aroused."[8]

The dossier went on to describe how "I" works and why it should be used. It was described as being tasteless and odourless. Drinking water, both hard and soft, is not visibly affected even when a lethal dose of 2g per 2.5 pints is reached.[9] When added to black coffee, there is no perceptible change in appearance, and this remains the case even if milk is added to it. There was some discussion about whether Hitler drank coffee and in what quantity.

Tea was a bit more problematic, because without milk, it would immediately become opalescent when thallium was added. It would show many points of shifting colours against a pale or dark background. In the course of an hour, the tea would become turbid – cloudy or opaque – and would show a brown sediment. Fortunately for the Foxley planners, their intelligence showed that Hitler preferred to drink his tea with milk. He was described as a "tea addict" and the milk was always poured first, meaning that the opalescence would not be seen.

The poison would similarly be undetectable in fruit, such as apples and prunes, that was stewed or boiled in water. Though little of the toxin would be absorbed by the fruit, the SOE dossier notes that "the juice would be lethal." The dossier added that the Führer was "extremely fond" of apple juice.

The appearance of beer would not be changed with the poison added to it, but wines and spirits became cloudy and produced a brown sediment, as happened with tea. Hitler was famously teetotal; he drank bottled water and what was called a "near beer". According to the file, "This beer is said to be a special product of the HOLZKIRCHEN brewery, Munich, whose lorry makes a delivery once a month to the Berghof."[10] SOE considered the possibility that this "near beer" might be poisoned, but decided it would be difficult.

John Emsley, in his book *Elements of Murder*, described how thallium works as a toxin. It is a cumulative poison, that works slowly like lead, attacking the nervous system. It was used for some time on children, to remove their hair in order to fight ringworm. It was also used as a poison against vermin. Water-soluble thallium salts are readily absorbed through the mouth, stomach and intestines, and can even penetrate the skin. A fatal dose of thallium is just 800mg for an adult – less than a quarter of a teaspoon, and considerably less than what SOE was planning to use against Hitler.

If SOE had managed to get thallium into Hitler's drinking water, the likely effect would have been as follows: initially, there would be no symptoms at all, or mild signs typical of a cold or flu. The next day, gastroenteritis (infectious diarrhoea) might set in. By the third day, the victim would experience "band-like pain around the body, joint pains, feet become very sensitive to touch, and sleep is almost impossible". Over time, the symptoms become much worse: muscles become paralysed, making it difficult to speak or swallow. The eyes become inflamed and the victim may go blind. A rash appears on the hands. In the end, victims of thallium poisoning are likely to die of respiratory disorders, pneumonia or heart failure.

The Perfect Murder

Thallium comes close to being the ideal poison for someone trying to get away with a "perfect murder". Thallium poisoning was often undetected, mistaken for other illnesses. It is extremely difficult to diagnose based on the symptoms alone, and this is true even after a post-mortem is carried out. "Typical autopsy findings are widespread degeneration of the peripheral nerve cells, but heart, intestines, liver, spleen, and pancreas may appear normal," Emsley wrote.[11]

Though a very good choice for murder, Thallium was not perfect. It had two major drawbacks: "The first one is that a victim will recover from a less-than-fatal dose and suffer hair loss, which would give the game away. The second is that forensic analysis can reveal its presence after death and even after cremation because some thallium migrates to the bones and is there retained."[12]

In addition, if a number of people on Hitler's train developed the same symptoms, having drunk the same water, it would have quickly become clear that poison had been used – though which poison may not have been obvious.

Though SOE may not have gotten its chance to use thallium against the Führer, its use has been contemplated by other regimes against other targets – perhaps most famously against Nelson Mandela. According to testimony given at a trial in South Africa in 2002, there had been a plan by the apartheid regime to poison Mandela back in 1990, the day before his release from prison. Thallium was the toxin they would have used, but thankfully decided not to do so.[13]

Saddam Hussein was apparently quite fond of thallium and used it against dozens of his enemies during the long years of his murderous rule in Iraq.[14]

Thallium therefore seemed well suited for the job of killing Hitler – and members of his entourage as well – on the *Führerzug*. But was "I" definitely thallium? Here the story gets a bit more complicated. "I" was identified as thallium acetate by someone who would almost certainly have known: Dr Paul Fildes. At first glance, Dr Fildes seemed an excellent source for this information. He has been described as "arguably Britain's foremost bacteriologist".[15]

But Fredric Boyce and Douglas Everett, authors of the authoritative *SOE: The Scientific Secrets*, had their doubts.[16] Boyce and Everett didn't fully trust Fildes' story. They hastened to point out that "there is no evidence to corroborate this story of substance 'I', nor is there any indication of how it was intended to administer the toxin."[17]

Why such distrust of an eminent expert on bacteriological warfare? This has little to do with Operation Foxley, the plan to assassinate Hitler, and is instead due to Operation Anthropoid, the assassination of Reinhard Heydrich in 1942. Decades after the event, there had been some speculation that Heydrich's death may have been caused by deliberate poisoning. This was because, although Heydrich was attacked by agents armed with Sten guns and grenades, he was not instantly killed. Instead, he survived for a full week in hospital, eventually falling into a coma and dying of blood poisoning.

Robert Harris and Jeremy Paxman wrote: "According to his own account, Paul Fildes made his most spectacular contribution to the Second World War on 27 May 1942 on a street corner in Prague in Czechoslovakia."[18]

Fildes had been working to weaponise botulinal toxins – using bacteria to cause people to develop botulism, a potentially fatal illness. The result was a toxin code-named "X". ("X" was not one of the poisons considered by SOE for Operation Foxley.) The hand grenades thrown at Heydrich were filled with "X" and he died because of the poison. Or so Fildes claimed. As Harris and Paxman wrote, Fildes told a number of his colleagues what he had done, saying that he "had a hand" in Heydrich's death. Fildes boasted to a young American biologist that Heydrich's murder "was the first notch on my pistol".[19]

But more recently, considerable doubts have been raised about Fildes' claim to have been responsible for Heydrich's death. M.R.D. Foot was quite clear about this. "Rumour has it that the grenade was poisoned," he wrote. "There is no need to believe this … the grenade fragments carried filth enough to kill him once embedded in his insides."[20] Scholars who have done recent work on the Heydrich killing share Foot's doubts about Dr Fildes' story, calling it "pure invention".[21]

If Fildes was an unreliable witness regarding the Heydrich killing, was he telling the truth about "I" actually being thallium acetate? We may never know.

— 5 —

The Manchurian Candidate

In a memo dated 8 July 1944, Air Commodore Archibald Boyle, SOE's Director of Intelligence, reviewed progress that had been made on Operation Foxley so far, and added a section with the headline "Foxley II?". This was just 10 days after the initial discussion in SOE about how to kill Hitler.

"It has been suggested", he wrote, "(and I seek direction on the point) that it will be advisable to couple Himmler with Hitler in the contemplated operation. Indeed, the abolition of Himmler would, in many respects, be more advantageous for reasons into which I need not go, and preparation of the necessary intelligence regarding the pair will be no more difficult than for individual treatment."[1]

It is clear that Boyle intended for Himmler to be killed when he was with Hitler, or nearby. Himmler was a regular visitor at Hitler's Alpine retreat near Berchtesgaden, which was the likely venue for an attack.

Five months after Boyle's memo, with nothing practical yet having been done, the subject of Foxley II came up again. This time it appeared in a memo marked "top secret" and sent by Major Leopold Herbert Manderstam to General Templer, head of the SOE's German Section X.

The Manchurian Candidate

Manderstam, whose SOE code name was "X/PLANS", was born in Riga, Latvia in July 1901. He studied at universities in the Soviet Union and Switzerland and for a brief time served in the Red Army. In the 1920s he moved to South Africa where he became a citizen. Manderstam was fluent in at least five languages and in March 1941 he joined SOE.

His career as an SOE agent was a colourful one, and he famously arranged to steal a Vichy French vessel from the harbour in Lobito, Angola, and to turn it over to the Royal Navy. His role in that operation earned him an MBE. Prior to taking on the role of X/PLANS, SOE used his knowledge of Russian to lead operations that included infiltrating Soviet agents into northern Italy.

Manderstam's short memo to Templer consisted of just five numbered sentences:

1. Has the possibility of using HESS for Foxley II ever been considered?
2. HESS might either be bluffed into doing it with the reason given to him that it might open a way for peace negotiations or, alternatively, be hypnotised into doing it.
3. HESS is known to be an extremely nervous individual and should be very susceptible to hypnotic treatment.
4. Has hypnotism ever been considered by us for our operations?
5. You are most probably aware of the success which an American Officer stationed in Ireland claims in this field?[2]

Major Manderstam was writing about Rudolf Hess, Hitler's former deputy who took a Luftwaffe plane and flew himself over to Britain on 10 May 1941 on what he described as a peace mission. Hess surrendered to British officers and had been held in captivity ever since.

Templer approved Manderstam's initial request for access to material on Hess, and on 8 January the latter submitted a more detailed questionnaire regarding Hess. Manderstam's questions included the following:

> Is Hess sane? If insane, is he subject to fits of insanity or is it of a more permanent nature? ... Can Hess be psychologically induced, by producing the necessary "evidence" into believing that Himmler, or any other Nazi leader, is the only person who prevents the re-approachment [sic] between Germany and Great Britain?[3]

Incredibly, by early 1945 discussion was taking place in the highest ranks in SOE about the possibility of "inducing" by means of hypnosis the former Deputy Führer to return to Germany and kill a top Nazi leader.

In a memoir written after the war, Manderstam indicated where his interest in hypnosis may have come from:

> Among the SOE officers at Bari was Captain A. R. (Dick) Cooper, a remarkable man ... and hypnotism was among his many skills. I was a sceptic, but I was converted when I saw him put some of our colleagues "under the influence". There was no trickery about it, yet when he tried to hypnotise me he failed. We both had strong wills and I could not relax sufficiently to allow another person to dominate my mind.[4]

In his own memoir of the period, *Adventures of a Secret Agent*, Dick Cooper wrote about his skills as a hypnotist. A prisoner in an enemy jail, he was once visited by a guard who suffered from toothache. Cooper suggested that he could ease the pain and the guard agreed to give him a chance to do so. "I started to hypnotize him," Cooper wrote.

> "Look well into my eyes," I murmured. "Relax completely. Breathe hard, breathe very hard. The pain is going. You are feeling a little sleepy now, but never mind, don't fight

against it because if you do the pain will return. The pain is gone now, but shut your eyes completely and don't think at all. You must sleep now, sleep, sleep, sleep. I order you to sleep." And asleep he was![5]

Cooper's attempt to break out of jail failed, but one can imagine how he would have impressed Major Manderstam. It was almost certainly Manderstam's encounters with Cooper, and the stories Cooper told, that led Manderstam to propose the hypnosis of Rudolf Hess.

When the Public Records Office (now The National Archives) published the Foxley dossier in 1998, they commissioned historian Mark Seaman to write the introduction. He was scathing about the proposal to use a hypnotised Rudolf Hess to assassinate a top Nazi leader. After describing Major Manderstam's short memo, Seaman characterised the Foxley II project as having "lurched into fantasy".[6]

He described the memo as "one of the most bizarre SOE memoranda ever written". In Seaman's view, Hess was "the least suitable of candidates to undertake the assassination of Himmler even if, as Manderstam suggested, he might be 'bluffed' or 'hypnotised' into undertaking the task."

Denis Rigden, author of *Kill the Führer: Section X and Operation Foxley,* agreed and described Manderstam's suggestion as "perhaps the most bizarre one ever asked by an SOE staff officer".[7] He added: "Hess had none of the qualities of an SOE agent. … Imagine him as an adviser to the German Directorate or as an 'escapee' or 'emissary' between Britain and Nazi Germany!" Rigden concluded that there was no evidence that Hess, "a die-hard Nazi, ever wished to play any sort of secret service role on the Allies' behalf".[8]

Other historians who have written about this tend to agree. Roger Moorhouse, in his book *Killing Hitler: The Third Reich and the Plots to Kill the Führer,* called the idea that "Hess might be persuaded (or even hypnotised) to return to Germany and play the role of an assassin" bizarre.[9]

Pretty much everyone who wrote about this proposal fell upon the same word to describe it: *bizarre.*

When the Foxley documents were made public, this part of the story was universally ridiculed. As the BBC put it, "Some of the proposals were clearly ludicrous, including the idea that Hitler's deputy Rudolf Hess, who was in gaol in the UK, should be hypnotised into killing Hitler."[10]

The proposal to hypnotise Hess and turn him into an assassin is eerily similar to the plot of *The Manchurian Candidate*, the 1959 novel by Richard Condon, turned into a Hollywood film in 1962 and again in 2004. *The Manchurian Candidate* was published at the height of the Cold War, and followed closely upon real events that took place during the Korean War. Several captured American servicemen made "confessions" to their North Korean and Chinese captors – confessions in which they admitted to, among other things, using bacteriological weapons. In the US, it was widely believed that the prisoners of war would never have made such statements voluntarily, and therefore they must have been "brainwashed". The term "brainwashing", now in common use, was initially used to describe techniques pioneered by the Chinese Communists. A CIA propagandist, Edward Hunter, made up the term from the Chinese *hsi-nao* – "to cleanse the mind". It caught on.[11]

In Condon's novel, he took things a step further. A fictional Chinese scientist named Yen Lo discovered a way to hypnotise prisoners and turn them into murderers. One of them, Sgt Raymond Shaw, was programmed to assassinate – eight years later – an American presidential candidate. Yen Lo lectured his Soviet and Chinese colleagues about how he was able to do this:

> I am sure that all of you have heard that old wive's tale …. which is concerned with the belief that no hypnotized subject may be forced to do that which is repellent to his moral nature, whatever that is, or to his own best interests. That is nonsense, of course.[12]

And to prove that there is a scientific foundation for what he was about to do, Yen then rattled off a number of scientific publications that provided the basis for his plan to create a hypnotised assassin:

> You note-takers might set down a reminder to consult Brenmen's [sic] paper, "Experiments in the Hypnotic Production of Antisocial and Self-injurious Behaviour" or Wells's 1941 paper which was titled, I believe, "Experiments in the Hypnotic Production of Crime", or Andrew Salter's remarkable book, *Conditioned Reflex Therapy* to name only three. Or, if it offends you to think that only the West is studying how to manufacture more crime and better criminals against modern shortages, I suggest Krasnogorski's *Primary Violence* or Serov's *The Unilateral Suggestion to Self-Destruction.* For any of you who are interested in massive negative conditioning there is Frederic Wertham's *The Seduction of the Innocent*, which demonstrates how thousands have been brought to antisocial actions through children's cartoon books. However, enough of that. You won't read them anyway.[13]

Authors often cite fictional sources to lend believability to their story. But the books and articles cited by the fictional Yen Lo seem to be, by and large, genuine. This is extraordinary. N.I. Krasnogorski, for example, was a disciple of Pavlov, and his writings were already available in English in the 1930s.[14] Brenman and Wells are of particular interest because they were published in mainstream English-language academic journals of psychology and psychiatry during the war.

Wesley Raymond Wells' article was published in the *Journal of Psychology* in 1941.[15] He was a professor of psychology at the University of Syracuse in upstate New York, and his article challenged conventional thinking about what could and could not be done by hypnosis.

"This investigation has been devoted to the problem of whether a hypnotized subject who is of non-criminal character can be made to commit real crime," he wrote. "The answer, on the basis of the actual experimental achievement of this result, is most emphatically in the affirmative."

Margaret Brenman's article was published in the journal *Psychiatry* during the following year.[16]

In other words, when Major Manderstam made his suggestion in December 1944 that Rudolf Hess might be hypnotised into becoming an assassin of Nazi leaders – and indeed asked if "hypnotism has ever been considered by us for our operations" – it may not have seemed such a crazy idea *at the time.* Based on his own personal experience with Captain Dick Cooper, and the fact that using hypnosis to induce criminal behaviour was the subject of serious academic research, Manderstam's suggestion may not have seemed bizarre or ludicrous.

Was it possible to hypnotise Rudolf Hess and send him back to Germany to kill Nazi leaders? Today, most would consider the idea absurd. But based on research by Wells, Brenman, Salter and others, this being the latest information available to SOE, it did seem to be something worth considering. And when one learns more about Rudolf Hess himself, the appeal of Manderstam's proposal becomes more apparent. Hess was a surprisingly suitable candidate for the role being proposed.

In Manderstam's original memo from December 1944, he wrote "HESS is known to be an extremely nervous individual and should be very susceptible to hypnotic treatment." That may or may not be true, but people who believe strongly in hypnosis often make better subjects (while some who are sceptical make quite poor subjects – as Manderstam and Cooper discovered).

It turns out that Rudolf Hess was *obsessed* with hypnosis, as his doctors discovered during his years of captivity in Britain. After the war, those doctors decided to publish a book based on their observations of Hess from the time of his capture in Scotland in 1941 until his transfer to the International Military Tribunal in Nuremberg. But they didn't want to publish the book without Hess' consent.

On 27 September 1946 Hess agreed to the publication of the medical reports, insisting only that his letter appear in the book "fully and literally". It appears on the first pages, in English translation and in the German original. Hess wrote:

> I would welcome it [the publication of the book] because one day it will be regarded as supplementary proof of the fact that in some hitherto unknown manner people can be put into a condition which resembles that which can be attained through a hypnosis leaving its after-effects ("post-hypnotic suggestion") – a condition in which the persons concerned do everything that has been suggested to them.[17]

Hess' obsessive references to hypnosis appeared throughout the book, starting with his capture in 1941. "The prisoner [Hess] confirmed in writing his suspicions that a number of the officers surrounding him were being hypnotised and used by an evil power to encompass his destruction," is one early reference.[18]

He continued to believe that those around him had been hypnotised:

> The eyes were the symptoms that the people around me had been put into an abnormal mental condition by a secret chemical which had been unknown to the world so far. The condition however is like a partial lunacy, or like a condition which might be created by hypnosis of long duration. In this condition, people can be made to behave like rogues or enemies towards someone for a certain time and to commit crimes such as murder. Then at a prefixed time, under hypnotic influence, they will get excited and will carry out what had been suggested to them.[19]

Hess was absolutely convinced that hypnosis was a powerful tool that was already being used by Germany's enemies. Indeed, he was convinced that it had been used against *him*. Near the end of the war, on 4 February 1945, he woke up much earlier than usual and displayed signs of agitation. He asked to see one of the doctors. As they recalled the conversation, it began like this: "he said that his memory had returned, and that he had something important to tell the world, and he asked that the information he was about to give should be forwarded to the Prime Minister."[20]

He then produced a sheet of paper with a list of names. The list included the King of Italy, the German officers who tried to kill Hitler the previous July, Winston Churchill and Hess himself. Hess explained the meaning of his list: "He stated that the Jews had 'some power' to hypnotise people without their being aware of any change in their personality, and that in this hypnotic state they did their misdeeds. All the above people mentioned had been thus hypnotised and he proceeded to enlarge about each of the names …" The King of Italy wouldn't have signed an armistice with the Allies, nor would the German officers have made an attempt on Hitler's life unless they had been hypnotised. Churchill, he believed, had switched over from being strongly anti-Bolshevik to being Stalin's ally – and only hypnosis could explain that.

The doctors described Hess' beliefs as part of his "delusional state". Hypnosis continued to play a role in this – for example, when Allied soldiers captured the strategically important Remagen bridgehead in March 1945. Hess explained this defeat in the only way he could: the German soldiers who were guarding the bridge, he announced, "had been hypnotised by the Jews".[21]

Based on what we now know about hypnosis, its potential and its limitations, it seems that Major Manderstam's idea would not have worked. Even had Hess been "programmed" to assassinate Nazi leaders, it was highly unlikely that he would have been given access to them if returned to Germany. Hitler and the other leaders of the Third Reich considered Hess to be insane or a traitor – or both.

But this was hardly the craziest idea in circulation as we shall see when reviewing later what SOE's American colleagues were thinking of doing.

Could It Have Worked?

In the years following the end of the Second World War, intelligence agencies continued to explore the use of hypnosis as a way to programme assassins. In the 1970s, when the CIA came under public scrutiny for its various covert (and sometimes illegal) Cold War shenanigans, the MKULTRA programme was revealed.[22]

The discovery of some of the fringe scientific research involved, including extensive use of lysergic acid diethylamide (LSD), caused a major scandal.

Conspiracy theorists speculated on the possibility that a "Manchurian candidate" was not only considered, but actually tried in practice. One candidate for that role was Sirhan Sirhan, who shot and killed Senator Robert F. Kennedy on 6 June 1968. Sirhan claimed to have no memory of having shot the Senator and never admitted his guilt. Investigators who used hypnosis on him later claimed that it was clear Sirhan had been hypnotised before.[23]

The British entertainer Derren Brown produced a television film in 2011 in which he attempted to replicate a Sirhan-style hypnotically induced assassination.[24] A volunteer was selected to be hypnotised as an assassin and duly opened fire on actor Stephen Fry in a London theatre. Unknown to the volunteer, the gun was loaded with blanks, and Fry – though not the audience – was in on the stunt.

Brown asked two academics for their views on whether someone could be hypnotically ordered to carry out a murder. Both were sceptical. Nearly a decade after Brown's film was shown, Professor Zoltan Dienes of the School of Psychology at the University of Sussex remains a sceptic. "I don't think it would work," he wrote. "When the experiment is done properly, people readily resist the hypnotic suggestion."[25]

Professor Stuart Derbyshire, now based at the Department of Psychology at the National University of Singapore, also had his doubts, despite the apparent success of Brown's stunt. "I would maintain that you cannot hypnotise somebody into committing an act that is against their conscience," he wrote. "The problem with the Derren Brown show was that Chris always knew he was taking part in a TV show and that there was no way he would ever be allowed to commit an actual criminal act. Thus his conscience was never in danger of being violated."

However, he added:

> That doesn't mean that hypnosis could not be used to create an assassin. Many harbour dark secrets, and it is perfectly within the bounds of many people's morality to commit some anti-social, immoral, or downright criminal and heinous acts. By 1944, it is quite conceivable that Hess saw Hitler as a problem and assassination as a solution. Involving him in some clandestine hypnotic plan could give him an excuse, if he wasn't particularly susceptible to hypnosis, or could gel with his conscience if he was.[26]

In his book, *Tricks of the Mind*, Derren Brown recounted how he first became interested in hypnosis. He described a show he attended in the early 1990s given by a hypnotist called Martin S. Taylor.[27] The formal demonstration of his powers was followed, Brown recalled, by an after-show session at a student's house. It was what Brown called his "Damascus experience". He decided then and there to become a hypnotist.[28]

Martin S. Taylor today continues to perform, describing what he does as "hypnotism without hypnosis". When informed about the SOE discussion regarding Rudolf Hess, he was not dismissive of the idea.[29]

Hypnosis, he explained, gives people an excuse to do what they would have done – it gives them moral permission. Being on stage, the pressure of the crowd, a desire to help or support the performer, all of these are factors. When someone is hypnotised on stage, they are aware of the fact that they are the centre of attention. Hypnosis plays with their subconscious motivation.

But could someone be hypnotised one day and made to act on it many weeks or months later? This is the premise of *The Manchurian Candidate* and it also the idea behind Major Manderstam's proposal to SOE in December 1944. Taylor answered in the affirmative. The bottom line, he said, is that this was not a *completely* crazy idea.

— 6 —

"Peace on Earth to All Men of Good Will"

Six months into the planning of Operation Foxley, little progress had been made into making it operational. Messages and memoranda had circulated about a sniper, poison and – soon – the use of hypnotised assassins. But it was all still a theoretical discussion.

The state of the plan to kill Hitler can be summarised most clearly in a memo sent on Christmas Day 1944 from Major General Templer, the head of SOE's Section X, to Colonel Francis Thomas Davies, the Director of Research, Development and Supplies.[1]

Tommy Davies, then 38 years old, had specialised in irregular warfare. Davies was described by colleagues as being ruthless and efficient.[2]

In his Christmas Day message, Templer thanked Davies for an earlier memo and noted that "you will be producing some beastlinesses in the next few weeks", though he went into no detail about them.

Templer explained that he had "personally ruled completely out of the argument any question of the infiltration of a body into the private apartments, kitchens or whatnot, of the person concerned. In view of the very high standard of security precautions which are undoubtedly carried out among the entourage, I cannot believe that we shall have any success along this line."

"Peace on Earth to All Men of Good Will"

In other words, if Hitler were to be shot or poisoned, it would not be by someone who had infiltrated his entourage. The alternative, he suggested, was "to stage some affair à la Heidrich [sic]". Presumably, what he meant was having an agent get close enough to the Führer to shoot him, or blow him up. "This presents no particular difficulty, certainly not on the equipment side, and the only snag is the production of the body to do the job. We are always looking for one – so far without any success." He presumably meant the recruitment of the sniper, which was proving quite difficult. As we saw, the potential assassin that SOE finally approached in early 1945, Captain Bennett, hardly seemed up to the task.

On Christmas Day, Templer was thinking about a sniper hiding in the forests around Berchtesgaden, waiting for his chance to shoot Hitler, as well as alternatives. Responding to questions which Tommy Davies had raised, he made clear that a whole range of options was still on the table. "If we can get permission to do the job I cannot believe that anyone will boggle at the use of chemicals. Let us say straight away that they are allowed," he wrote. "The same remarks apply as to the use of bacteria."

He then addressed the critical question of how to extricate the SOE's agent after he had done the job. "I cannot say whether I envisage the operation as a suicide one or not," he wrote. "If the body is going to use some method which will do the trick more or less instantaneously and which he will be spotted doing, then it is obviously a suicide. This may not be the case. It depends on what you produce." Davies' team could produce quite a range of toxins, some of which did not work instantly, such as thallium.

Thinking about where Hitler would be killed, Templer imagined options that did not involve a sniper in the woods. He anticipated that killing Hitler using a chemical or biological weapon would take place in "an office, so to speak, inside a private house". There would likely be what later came to be called "collateral damage". "Others will probably be present in the room," he wrote, "though probably only one or two."

The important thing, he emphasised, was to ensure that Hitler was killed. If that happened, he concluded, "I do not mind whether it is attributable to natural causes or attack." He ended the message by noting that "in view of the date, I should like to add 'peace on earth to all men of good will'."

— 7 —

Combined Operation

Of all the ideas proposed in the Operation Foxley dossier, only one seems to have been attempted in practice – a "combined operation".

The idea of combined operations was to bring together the Royal Air Force, the Royal Navy and the Army, usually in commando strikes against the Germans. While this was mostly done on a small scale, the disastrous raid on Dieppe in August 1942 showed that a combined operation could also mean deploying thousands of men. Of course Operation Overlord, the Normandy landings on 6 June 1944, was a very successful example of combined operations in practice.

Operation Foxley imagined a scenario in which it became known that Hitler was in residence at the Obersalzberg and a combined operation might be launched involving an aerial bombardment of the Führer's home and the SS barracks nearby. This would be accompanied by the dropping of a paratroop battalion from the Special Air Service (SAS). The report says that such an attack "would be well worth while since it offers the best chance of eliminating the Führer as well as the other leading Nazies [sic] in the OBERSALZBERG, Martin BORMANN, for instance".

Just as the Foxley dossier seems somewhat over-optimistic regarding the chances of success for the other proposed actions, including a sniper or the use of poison, in this case the SOE again anticipated a relatively easy victory. As the dossier explained, "there would be little opposition" to such a raid. The Germans would deploy their anti-aircraft guns against the RAF planes and their special machines would create a covering of smoke over the whole complex to make it difficult for the bombers. But the men of the RSD and other forces protecting Hitler would certainly "take to the air raid shelters in all probability" leaving only a skeletal force above ground. These would include the fire-fighting platoon, the guards at the entrances to the air raid shelters, and those lightly armed soldiers specifically designated to fight against Allied troops. "A paratroop battalion could therefore swamp any resistance the troops guarding the OBERSALZBERG might put up," the dossier concludes.

The Foxley planners believed that it was unlikely any help could arrive from elsewhere. There might have been garrisons in nearby towns like Salzburg, but these may well have been sent to the front. And the RAF bombers could make the deployment of reinforcements difficult by extending their bombing raid to cover those towns too. Reading the proposal in light of what we know about the difficulties of airborne attacks – difficulties that were common knowledge by 1945 – this seems rather over-optimistic, and even cocky.

The idea of a combined operation attack on Hitler's Alpine retreat was apparently shelved because it was thought this would be best timed to coincide with an uprising by foreign workers in the Salzburg area. The dossier mentions plans to use French deportees, prisoners of war, Poles and *Ostarbeiter* (forced labourers from Eastern Europe) who would have seized the arms depot in Salzburg. But this plan never came into being because of a lack of cooperation with the "foreign governments" (presumably the London-based governments in exile).

Even though the dossier ends its discussion of the combined operation on that note, the idea of bombing the Obersalzberg was not forgotten. On the night of 25 April 1945, just five days before

Combined Operation

Hitler took his own life in Berlin, the RAF launched a massive raid on Berchtesgaden. In one of the last such raids of the war, 375 bombers were unleashed against the Obersalzberg. Two of them were shot down, with a loss of four men. Six Germans died on the ground and the complex was severely damaged. Among the buildings hit were the homes of Göring and Bormann, though neither of them was in the area at the time. The SS barracks and the RSD garrison were also damaged. The Berghof, Hitler's home, was hit too. But the proposed deployment of a battalion of SAS soldiers did not take place.

Roger Moorhouse speculated on what motivated the British to carry out that raid, so close to the end of the war. "One has to wonder," he asked, "what military rationale would induce the RAF to target a few buildings in a remote area of south-east Germany with a force of 375 aircraft?" Maybe it was a belated attempt to kill Hitler.

Or maybe it was an attempt to disrupt the rumoured "Alpine Redoubt" where it was feared that the Nazis might make a last stand after the fall of Berlin. Two months earlier, the SOE's Captain James Joll suggested that "it seems reasonably probable that the majority of such people" – high-ranking Nazis – "will eventually retire to the Berchtesgaden–Salzburg area for their final stages of the war." Any SOE agents in place in the area might want to target them for assassination.[1]

Moorhouse concluded, "It may just be that the enormous raid on Berchtesgaden was merely the result of a fit of pique. It was, perhaps, a demonstration of what might have been done earlier, had circumstances, tactical considerations – and scruples – allowed."[2]

Meanwhile, Britain's allies were also considering ways to kill the German Führer.

— 8 —

Stalin's "Hitler Scheme"

The first of Britain's wartime allies to plot the assassination of Adolf Hitler was probably the Soviet Union. From the very earliest days of the Nazi Party, Hitler was a sworn enemy of the German Communists and of the Soviet Union. The Soviet leadership was aware of this, and after Hitler came to power in 1933, it anticipated a war with Germany. In addition to public activity opposing the Nazi regime, Soviet intelligence services operating abroad were open to the possibility of killing the German leader even before the outbreak of war.

Though SOE never managed to get a sniper anywhere near Hitler, the first of the Soviet plans to kill the Führer would ironically have relied on a pair of British men. In early 1939, Alexander Allan Foote, a British-born agent of the Glavnoye Razvedyvatelnoye Upravlenie (GRU) – Soviet Military Intelligence – spotted an opportunity.

Foote was "tall and a bit overweight. His hair was a reddish blonde, the eyelashes were fair, complexion pale and eyes blue. His appearance was very acceptable and he knows how to behave."[1] That description comes from his handler, Ursula Kuczynski, a German Jewish woman who had done outstanding work as a Soviet spy in China, Japanese-occupied Manchuria, and Poland. Kuczynski was now based in Switzerland where she worked for the GRU.

Stalin's "Hitler Scheme"

Foote was sympathetic to the Communist cause, but not a Party member.[2] Like many others, he volunteered to fight against Franco in Spain and served in the British Battalion of the 6th International Brigade. He stayed in Spain for two years. Upon his return to Britain in the autumn of 1938, he was recruited to the GRU and told to report to Geneva, where he would meet his handler. When Kuczynski met Foote, she ordered him to report to Munich and to "keep his eyes and ears open, seek acquaintances among Nazis and, if possible, establish connections with the Messerschmidt aeroplane factory".[3] He was given no instructions regarding Hitler.

But by chance, Foote stumbled upon an extraordinary opportunity. "I lit by accident on Hitler's *Stammtisch*," he later wrote, using the German word for an informal gathering. "Looking one day for a cheap place to lunch, I found by accident the Osteria Bavaria on Schellingstrasse, and, having settled down to the good 1s. 6d. set lunch, I noticed a flurry at the door." The flurry marked the entrance of the German dictator, "accompanied by his adjutant Bruecker, his photographer and toady Hoffmann, and two A.D.C.s".[4]

Foote later learned that the owner of the restaurant was an old comrade of Hitler's. The Führer ate lunch in his restaurant every time he was in Munich, as often as three times a week. He always ordered the same food: eggs and mayonnaise, vegetables and pasta, fruit compote or a raw apple. He also always drank *"Fachinger Wasser,"* a mineral water which he believed could neutralise excessive acid in the stomach.

Foote told his handler Kuczynski what he had seen. "What an excellent idea," she said. "She sent my report back over her secret transmitter to the Director" in Moscow, he later wrote. "I was told that the Director was extremely interested in the report on Hitler and instructed me to check up on his movements and habits."[5]

In April 1939, Foote was joined in Munich by another Spanish Civil War veteran who was one of Kuczynski's spies (and future husband), Len Beurton. Beurton told Foote that he had been ordered to help with what was now called the "Hitler scheme". This surprised Foote, who had received only vague instructions to keep an eye on the Nazi leader. But things had moved on.

In the two months since he had told Kuczynski of this extraordinary opportunity "the idea had burgeoned in the mind of the Kremlin into a full-blown scheme for assassination, with Bill [Beurton's code name] and myself apparently cast for the principal rôles."

Foote suggested to Beurton that they lunch at the Osteria Bavaria that day in order to have a look at Hitler from up close. As Hitler entered the restaurant, they were told to stub out their cigarettes, as the Führer could not tolerate smoking. All the other customers rose to give the Hitler salute. The two Soviet spies were not obliged to join in, but they did stand up with everyone else. Two women were waiting for Hitler in the restaurant. One was Unity Mitford, the Führer's number one fan in Britain, and the other was his mistress, Eva Braun. As Hitler moved through the restaurant he was greeted with loud applause.

Foote was not enthusiastic about the possibility that he was going to have to give up his life in an attempt on Hitler. "We were neither of us very willing actors, as neither of us really fancied a martyr's crown – especially as on the face of it the scheme appeared suicidal and doomed to failure." He added that "we did feel, however, that in fairness to our employers, who, after all, had been paying us for some months with little or no return for their money, it behove us to look into the matter – and the result was not unpromising."[6]

Beurton, on the other hand, *loved* the idea. "What could be easier than to put a time bomb in an attaché case along with our coats and, having had an early lunch, abandon the lot in the hope that the bomb would blow Hitler and his entourage … into eternity?"[7]

Foote learned more about the Führer's habits. "Hitler always lunched in a private room, which was only separated by a thin wooden partition from the corridor leading from the restaurant to the lavatories." That partition was used to hang customers' coats. It appeared to the two GRU men that "there was no special surveillance of the place, and no extra precautions were put into force when the Fuehrer honoured it with his presence."[8] The lax security surrounding Hitler in the run-up to the war has been noted by others.

Foote came up with a plan: a time bomb in an attaché case next to that partition. That was it – that was the whole plan. Instead of Operation Foxley's months of research, interviews with countless captured Germans, sketches of the Obersalzberg's floor layouts and carefully rendered full-colour images of how his bodyguards dressed and the uniforms they wore, Foote's scheme was that simple – a bomb in a restaurant.

"Neither of us believed in the effectiveness of terrorist attacks on individuals," Kuczynski wrote. "But there were some people we considered so dangerous and bestial that we were both prepared to break the rules." While staying at her home in Switzerland, the two men practised making bombs.

Years later, reflecting back on it, Foote wrote that "it appears to me to have been well-nigh fool-proof. It also bears a startling resemblance to the July, 1944 attempt by Stauffenberg."[9] Based on what Foote had learned later about the failed July 1944 plot, his 1939 attempt might have worked. "We were too innocent then to know the niceties of explosives, but as the other three walls were solid Bavarian stone it seems likely that we might have been successful," he wrote.[10]

It was not the only plan Foote came up with. A second plan "involved assassination in its more traditional character – by revolver rather than T.N.T." As the two Britons had learned, when the Nazi leader would enter the Osteria Bavaria, he habitually acknowledged the plaudits of the diners, who would rise to their feet when he entered the room. Foote and Beurton decided to try something out. Beurton "stationed himself at the table next to the gangway, and as Hitler approached put his hand rapidly and furtively into his pocket – and drew out a cigarette case," Foote recalled. "I on the other side of the room watched the reactions of Hitler's entourage and the rest of the lunchers, among whom, one imagined, there must have been a fair sprinkling of trigger-happy Gestapo agents."

They were expecting the worst. They had assumed that the room was full of secret agents guarding the Führer. No one knew then how lax the security was at that time.

"Nothing whatever happened" when Beurton reached into his pocket, Foote remembered. "No reaction was visible, though to my heated imagination no action could have looked more suspicious. Looking back on this, it all seems incredibly amateurish, even though Bill's act required a considerable amount of personal courage."[11]

In May 1939, Foote met Kuczynski in Switzerland. She ordered him to continue preparations for the assassination of Hitler. He agreed, but later claimed that he had no intention of doing further research. "All that was necessary was an explosive suitcase or a potential suicide, and Sonia's network could provide neither," he later wrote.[12]

The two British men were physically closer to Hitler than any other Allied assassins ever got, they had a workable plan, they were trained in bomb-making and they had a target who was barely defended. If there was ever a good time to assassinate Hitler, the summer of 1939 was it. War was imminent. Hitler was not yet surrounded by an army of bodyguards. He could still wander into his favourite restaurant, ordering his *Fachinger Wasser* while armed Soviet spies sat only a few tables away. Those spies had the means, motive and opportunity to carry out the plan. All they needed was a green light from Moscow.

Instead, Kuczynski received an urgent message from Moscow ordering her to "pull all the agents she could out of Germany and break all contact with any remaining resident agents".[13] As Kuczynski put it in her memoir, "political events overtook us and eliminated this possibility" of killing Hitler.[14] Those "political events" consisted of the Molotov–Ribbentrop Pact, signed on 23 August 1939.

In the blink of an eye, Hitler was no longer a target for assassination by Soviet agents. Nazi Germany was no longer the Soviet Union's mortal enemy and its leader, Adolf Hitler, was now a trusted ally of Stalin. The GRU's "Hitler scheme" was abandoned.

Stalin's "Hitler Scheme"

Unlike the SOE's Operation Foxley, this "Hitler scheme" would have killed the German dictator several months *before* the outbreak of the Second World War, possibly averting a catastrophe and saving millions of lives. And the chance of success was never better than in 1939 when security around the Führer was lax and Hitler's whereabouts were well known.

The Soviet–German alliance lasted less than two years. Once Hitler's armies invaded the USSR on 22 June 1941, the assassination of the Führer was once again on the table. "I am extremely anxious to see Hitler dead," a furious Stalin was quoted as saying.[15] But by this time Kuczynski and her agents were no longer in place, and the Soviet intelligence services would have to come up with a better plan.

One of the first plans was based on the belief that the rapid German advance in the first months of the 1941 invasion would lead to the capture of Moscow. On the assumption that Hitler would visit the Soviet capital to celebrate his triumph there – as he had done in Vienna and Paris – it was decided to plant mines in the Bolshoi theatre and blow it up when Hitler would visit there. The agent in charge of this plan, Pavel Sudoplatov, was a well-known saboteur. The only reason the attempt wasn't made was that the Wehrmacht never reached Moscow.

The following year, Stalin was "extremely keen to know of Hitler's whereabouts and pestered the British in the spring of 1942 with requests for the relevant intelligence" according to Roger Moorhouse.[16]

The second plan that Sudoplatov was involved in aimed to kill Hitler at his Wehrwolf headquarters near Vinnitsa, where a partisan detachment led by Dmitri Medvedev, a veteran NKVD officer, was sent. This plan was codenamed "Munich" for some reason – ironically, as the best chance the Soviets had was the earlier scheme to blow Hitler up in his favourite restaurant in the Bavarian city.

Medvedev had been working behind German lines for some time. He began looking into conducting a "special action" at Wehrwolf in the spring of 1943. His men claimed to have seen Hitler there, travelling in a limousine. But they missed their chance. Hitler left Vinnitsa in March 1943, returning only once later that year for a short visit.

Thwarted in their plans to killer Hitler in Munich in 1939, in Moscow in 1941 and in Vinnitsa in 1943, the Soviet security services reached the conclusion that the assassination of Hitler would have to take place in Berlin.

This was a more complicated and difficult operation than blowing up a restaurant in Munich, or the Bolshoi theatre in Moscow. It would require "meticulous planning, watertight cover stories and, most important, a well-placed contact to engineer a meeting between the Führer and his would-be assassin," wrote Moorhouse.[17]

The person chosen for the task was Lev Knipper. A former White Russian émigré and nephew of the playwright Anton Chekhov, Knipper may also have been involved with the early plan to assassinate Hitler in Moscow. Knipper had several things going for him: he could pass as an Aryan and spoke fluent German. And he had a great contact in Berlin – his older sister, Olga Chekhova. Olga had become a successful actor, appearing in over 100 films. She was a part of the Nazi cultural elite, sometimes dining with Goebbels. She was once photographed with Hitler, as the Führer kissed her hand, leading some to believe that a romantic relationship existed between the two. Chekhova was also an NKVD sleeper agent who could be activated as needed by the Soviets.

Her brother Lev was sent to Iran to prepare for his "defection" to the Germans. The plan was for him to travel to Berlin where he'd contact both his sister Olga and fellow NKVD agent Igor Miklashevsky, who had also "defected" to the Germans. Olga would somehow get Lev or Igor close to Hitler.

It was not a well-thought-out plan, and like all the others never became operational. This was because by 1943 the Führer no longer went to the kinds of events where he would meet actresses like Chekhova. In fact, Olga had not seen Hitler since 1940.

In any event, Stalin cancelled this plan as he had done the previous ones. According to Moorhouse, killing Hitler in 1943 "could even prove counterproductive [Stalin believed], leading to a revitalisation of the German military and, possibly, a separate peace with the Western Allies, leaving the USSR to fight on alone".[18]

The Soviets had at least three plans to kill Hitler, possibly several more. It is unlikely that we will ever know much about them, as no equivalent document to the Operation Foxley dossier has ever been published by Moscow.

The Soviet plans we do know about seemed quite realistic compared to some of the ideas floating around in SOE. But Hitler's life was spared on these occasions by decisions taken by his one-time ally and fellow dictator, Josef Stalin.

— 9 —

"Professor Moriarty"

SOE officers and the Soviet secret services were not alone in looking into the possibility of killing Adolf Hitler. Their American counterparts, the Office of Strategic Services (OSS) – forerunner of the CIA – was thinking about the same thing. It was also coming up with many of the same ideas, some of them as outlandish as the British ones – and some even more so.

The head of OSS, William J. "Wild Bill" Donovan, hired a Boston industrialist and Cornell University graduate named Stanley Lovell to head up a research and development team. When Lovell met Donovan for the first time, he was told: "Professor Moriarty is the man I want for my staff here at OSS. I think you're it." Donovan explained further what he meant: "I need every subtle device and every underhanded trick to use against the Germans and the Japanese … You're going to have to invent all of them, Lovell, because you're going to be my man."

Lovell's "job basically consisted of puttering around in a lab and thinking up cool spy tools," wrote journalist Sam Kean. His team:

> developed bombs that looked like mollusks to attach to ships. They crafted shoes and buttons and batteries with secret cavities to conceal documents. They invented

pencils and cigarettes that shot bullets. They devised an explosive powder called Aunt Jemima with the consistency of flour that could be mixed with water and even baked into biscuits and nibbled on without any danger; only when ignited with a fuse did Aunt Jemima detonate.[2]

Donovan's "Moriarty" strongly believed that the OSS should kill the German leader. "I had repeatedly pointed out in O.S.S. staff meetings the often-forgotten fact that the great advantage a democracy possessed over any dictatorship was the government's relative invulnerability, as opposed to the terrific risks inherent in any one-man rule," he later wrote. "Lop off the head and the body falls."[3]

The OSS learned that Hitler and Mussolini would soon be meeting at the Brenner Pass, on the border between Italy and Austria. Lovell thought that this was a great opportunity. "With Hitler and Mussolini dead, it would be safe to predict chaos or, at the very least, a murderous scramble for their empty chairs," he wrote.[4] But he didn't like the plan proposed, which he described like this: "Let us parachute a cadre of our toughest men into the area and shoot up the bastards! Sure, it'll be a suicide operation, but that's what we're organised to carry out."[5]

Lovell's plan, in the spirit of Arthur Conan Doyle's fictional criminal mastermind Moriarty, was more devious. OSS would place an agent in the room where the two dictators were scheduled to meet. The agent would need less than five minutes to place a vase with cut flowers in water on the conference table. The agent would then place a capsule containing liquid nitrogen-mustard gas into the water. The effect would be to permanently blind everyone in the room.[6]

Lovell suggested that the Allies get the Pope to issue a papal bull or something similar before Hitler and Mussolini met, to warn that evil leaders would soon be blinded by God. If that happened, German and Italian soldiers, or at least the Catholic ones, would clearly see that the dictators were evil men, and would rise up in mutiny, or refuse to fight. "Wild Bill" Donovan *loved* the idea. As he told the participants in the meeting, "You see, Gentlemen, why we have so depraved an idea man as Professor Moriarty on the staff!"[7] But Lovell's plan wasn't attempted because the date and venue of the fascist leaders' summit was changed.

This was *not* a plan to kill Hitler. That would come later. Lovell strongly believed that assassination was "a new way for America to wage a war," adding that "you win the game much faster if you checkmate the King and treat the pawns as the relatively unimportant nuisances they are."[8]

Instead of going for the sniper or bomb route, as both SOE and the various German resistance plotters had considered, Lovell instead insisted on what he called the "glandular approach". Donovan wanted a psychologist to write up an analysis of Hitler, something that OSS could use. They found Walter Langer, who taught psychology at Harvard University. Langer was asked to draft a report, which was later published as *A Psychological Analysis of Adolf Hitler: His Life and Legend*.

Obviously, Professor Langer was not able to meet Hitler face to face, and therefore based his report solely on what could be learned from secondary sources. Some of his conclusions may strike us today as being rather bizarre. For example, he wrote: "Many writers and informants have commented on his [Hitler's] feminine characteristics – his gait, his hands, his mannerisms and ways of thinking."[9]

In addition to noting the Führer's "feminine" thought processes, Langer added that "even today Hitler derives pleasure from looking at men's bodies and associating with homosexuals. [Otto] Strasser tells us that his personal body guard is almost always 100% homosexuals."[10]

Langer made several observations about possible Allied attempts on Hitler's life. He noted that Hitler "has a pathological fear of poisoning by mouth".[11] He was also very concerned that the Allies must not be seen to be the ones killing the Führer – a concern SOE shared in its planning for Operation Foxley. "This possibility too would be undesirable from our point of view inasmuch as it would make a martyr of him and strengthen the legend," he wrote.[12]

But it was Langer's analysis of Hitler's "feminine" characteristics that gave Lovell an idea for how to attack the German leader. "America's top diagnosticians and gland experts agreed with me that he [Hitler] was definitely close to the male–female line," Lovell explained. As evidence of this, he cited the Führer's "poor emotional control, his violent passions, his selection of companions like [homosexual SA boss Ernst] Röehm [sic], all led me to feel that a push to the female side might do wonders". Lovell was quite specific about what those "wonders" might consist of: "The hope was that his moustache would fall off and his voice become soprano."

It might be argued that, like the planned blinding at the Brenner Pass, this was not actually a plan to kill Hitler, even if Lovell discussed it within that framework. Lovell went into considerable detail about how the OSS might push Hitler "to the female side". He knew that Hitler was a vegetarian and that at Berchtesgaden there would have been a vegetable garden. Lovell's idea was to either infiltrate an OSS agent or use an anti-Nazi gardener. The plan – incredibly – was approved.

"I supplied female sex hormones and, just for variety's sake, now and then a carbamate or other quietus medication, all to be injected into der Führer's carrots, beets or whatever went up to his larder," Lovell recalled.[13]

But the plan evidently failed. "Since he survived, I can only assume that the gardener took our money and threw the syringes and medications into the nearest thicket. Either that or Hitler had a big turnover in his 'tasters'."

There is some confusion here, as either Lovell is discussing a plan to feminise the Nazi leader or to kill him – possibly both. If the former, a number of the Führer's "tasters" may have lost their facial hair or became sopranos. But there is no documentary evidence of this having occurred. Compared to this plan to "feminise" the German Führer, SOE's musings about hypnotising Rudolf Hess seem absolutely grounded in the real world.

Lovell and the OSS had another idea: there was a theory going around that Hitler was an epileptic. "We made a study of how to accelerate the disease or, conversely, overcome it [and] hopefully get Herr Schickelgruber[14] down to normalcy," wrote Lovell. "Nothing came of it, but again we tried."

While some of these ideas were unique to Lovell, occasionally the OSS and SOE's ideas would overlap, even though there is no evidence that OSS was aware of Operation Foxley or that SOE knew about the Americans' plans to turn Hitler into a soprano. One of those plans, Lovell explained, featured hypnosis: "We hoped to so indoctrinate a German [prisoner], posthypnotically, that if we smuggled him into Berlin or Berchtesgaden, he would assassinate Hitler in that posthypnotic state, being under a compulsion that might not be denied."[15]

The idea that someone could be programmed using hypnosis to kill Hitler was thus not unique to SOE's Major Manderstam. The main difference between what OSS was considering and the British plan was that the latter focussed on high-value Nazi targets in general, while the Americans thought it could be used specifically against Hitler.

Lovell decided to ask the experts if it could be done. He contacted:

> New York psychiatrist Lawrence Kubie and from the famed Menninger brothers, Karl and William. The Menningers reported that the weight of the evidence showed hypnotism to be incapable of making people do anything that they would not otherwise do. Equally negative, Dr Kubie added that if a German prisoner had a logical reason to kill Hitler or anyone else, he would not need hypnotism to motivate him.[16]

While Kubie and the Menninger brothers cautioned against the idea, there were others in the psychological profession in the US who thought it worth a second look. In addition to the researchers mentioned earlier – Wells, Brenman, Salter and Krasnogorski – there was the head of the Psychology Department at Colgate University in upstate New York, George "Esty" Estabrooks. "Since the early 1930s," wrote John Marks, "Estabrooks had periodically ventured out from his sleepy upstate campus to advise the military on applications of hypnotism."[17]

Unlike the SOE's Major Manderstam, who was enthusiastic about the possibility of hypnotising Hess, Lovell was sceptical. He believed what Kubie and the Menningers had told him. But he was willing to be persuaded. "I was understandably a bit cynical", he wrote, "when Colonel Buxton invited me to meet a hypnotist in his office – one who alleged he was a master of post-hypnotic suggestion."[18]

Lovell was not impressed with the "gentleman from South Carolina" who hypnotised two soldiers. Lovell was convinced that the soldiers – who he described as being "right off some impoverished South Carolina farm" – were playing along. The plan to send a hypnotised assassin to Nazi Germany was quietly shelved. In the years following the war, however, Estabrooks managed to persuade the CIA to run some experiments on creating hypnotised assassins, with intriguing results.

The American plans to kill Hitler did not end with beets and carrots or hypnotised assassins. They also contemplated somewhat more conventional approaches to killing the German dictator. At the very end of the war, they were considering a final attempt on Hitler's life. This strange episode involved the Soviet spy Ursula Kuczynski who we met earlier.

By 1945, Kuczynski was instrumental in selecting individuals to be parachuted into Germany to engage in covert operations. Two of the agents she sent to Berlin, Paul Lindner and Anton Ruh, were instructed by the OSS to determine Hitler's precise whereabouts "with a view to killing the Führer himself in a surgical bombing strike".[19]

Unlike the RAF's own belated raid on the Obersalzberg described in chapter 8, this mission was at least aimed at a place where Hitler could be found – Berlin. The only thing that prevented it from happening was Hitler's decision a few days later to take his own life.

Conclusion

When debating whether or not to kill Hitler, SOE had to answer several questions, including how to do it, who would do it, and when. But they also needed to determine what was likely to be the result of a successful attempt on Hitler's life. In other words, they worked with a number of "what-if" scenarios.

Their debates were serious and lasted over many months. Had Operation Foxley moved from the planning stages to an actual attack in 1944 or 1945, and had that attack succeeded, there were at least three foreseeable outcomes.

1. There is an immediate collapse of the German Reich and the end of the war.
This would have been the best result from the Allied point of view and this is precisely what the proponents of Operation Foxley were counting on. Indeed, this is what happened when Hitler finally took his own life on 30 April 1945. Though he designated Admiral Karl Dönitz as his successor, Hitler's death meant the sudden and complete collapse of the German armed forces.

As Ian Kershaw wrote in his foreword to *Operation Foxley*, the impact of Hitler's death on the war effort would have depended on *when* he was killed. Hitler's death early in the war, or indeed even

Conclusion

before the war broke out, would have had a major impact. Because the planning for Operation Foxley did not begin until after the Allied landings in Normandy, we need only consider the likely results of Hitler's sudden death on a Germany that was already facing certain defeat, during the final year of the war. This was particularly true by early 1945, when SOE was still searching for a sniper, exploring the use of chemical and bacteriological weapons, and discussing the possible use of Rudolf Hess as a "Manchurian candidate" hypnotically programmed to kill Nazi leaders.

It seems likely that Hitler's death in 1945 – whether by an SOE gunman, or the deliberate bombing of his compound at Berchtesgaden, or even by his own hand (as eventually happened) – would have speeded up the war's end.

2. A more competent leader takes charge, prolonging the war.
The outcome of the war from June 1944, when Foxley was first proposed, was in no doubt. The Normandy landings had been carried out successfully, the Allies were moving up the Italian peninsula, and Soviet forces were closing in on the Reich from the east. Even Japan was moving inexorably towards defeat. There was little doubt that the world war would end in a complete Allied victory.

No new German leader could have changed that, not even the most competent one. However, a new leader could have avoided *some* of Hitler's mistakes, and thereby have prolonged the war. For example, ditching the wasteful and doomed Ardennes offensive of December 1944 and instead using all of Germany's military strength to defend the Reich, especially on the eastern front, *might* have delayed the collapse of the German armed forces.

Himmler or Göring would almost certainly have taken power had Hitler been killed. Göring had failed utterly in his role as head of the Luftwaffe, and was a huge disappointment to Hitler because of that. Himmler, a murderous and sadistic head of the security forces, showed no competence at all as a military leader in the field. Neither of them could have reversed Germany's fortunes.

There were of course competent military leaders on the German side who might have held off the Allies longer without Hitler's interference. But those military leaders were unlikely to have stepped in to seize control upon his death. After the failed 20 July 1944 Stauffenberg plot, Germany's generals, cowed by the bloody reprisals against the conspirators, showed no further inclination to challenge the Nazi leadership. Even a military coup could not have led to a German victory. It was too late for that.

3. A new German leadership emerges that reaches out for a separate peace with the Western Allies.

Throughout the latter stages of the war, a separate peace between one or more of the Western Allies and the Germans was the Nazi dream – and Stalin's nightmare. Goebbels' diary entries in 1945 reflected his hope that the wartime alliance between the Soviet Union and the capitalist West was doomed to break up. He was not wrong about this, but his timing was off.

By the final weeks of the war, Nazi leaders such as Himmler were keen to have a separate peace with the Western Allies, and reached out through back channels to achieve this. That they did this even while Hitler was still alive gives an indication of what might have happened had he suddenly died. There is no evidence that the Western Allies were ever open to a separate peace with the Nazis, having committed themselves at the Casablanca Conference in January 1943 to the unconditional surrender of all German forces on all fronts

If an SOE sniper had succeeded in killing Hitler, or its agents had managed to poison the Führer with thallium acetate, and if this had allowed a new German government to reach out to the Western Allies for a separate peace, the Allies would not have agreed to it. And with the end of the war so near, they had no incentive to do so.

A missed opportunity
On balance, the successful assassination of Hitler at any point – before or during the war – would probably have shortened the

Conclusion

conflict and saved lives. The moral case for killing the Nazi leader was clear. As historian Franklin L. Ford wrote in his book *Political Murder: From Tyrannicide to Terrorism*: "The century's greatest single instance of tyrannicide ... would have been the assassination of Adolf Hitler. A target with clearer credentials for extinction would be difficult for anyone but the most thoroughly brainwashed Nazi to imagine."

One of the problems facing any plan to kill Hitler was the fact that there had already been many attempts and they had all failed. The 20 July 1944 plan probably came closest to success, managing to wound the Führer and kill several of his associates. But while some of the plans came close to fruition, all were stymied by the many powerful layers of security that surrounded the increasingly paranoid Hitler – as well as his remarkable luck. Could SOE have succeeded with a single sniper where so many others had failed?

At first glance, looking over the entire Operation Foxley dossier, one cannot help but feel that this was at best a half-hearted effort. For SOE, the most likely means of killing Hitler – using a sniper hiding in a forest to shoot him on his morning walk – seems to be inspired by a Hollywood movie and the British thriller it was based on. Like the film, not much thought was given to how a sniper might get into place, or how he would be safely extracted from the scene. In fact, the only real difference between the Foxley plan and *Man Hunt* was the idea that the assassin might wear a German uniform. The proposal to have a second team in place, armed with a bazooka or a PIAT gun, completely contradicted the plan to send in a German-speaking sniper, wearing a Wehrmacht uniform and carrying a Mauser rifle. Why go to such lengths to conceal the fact that the killer was British – and yet have others in place armed with that quintessential British weapon, the PIAT?

The dossier discussed in some detail different ways to poison the Führer. It seemed that the best one was to slip some thallium acetate into his drinking water on his train, the *Führerzug*. Who would do this, and how, was not seriously explored. And the use of thallium acetate, which SOE planners imagined would result in a "perfect murder" with no one knowing how it was done or by whom, seems more suited to an Agatha Christy "cozy" than to a real-world military operation.

In this context, some of the more outlandish ideas seem to fit right in. These were not serious proposals but rather brainstorming, where any idea, however crazy, could be put on the table. As Roger Moorhouse concluded, "Foxley was still very much a planning document, a feasibility study, drawn up from behind a desk in London's Baker Street. The enormous gulf between planning and operation had yet to be bridged."[2]

In the end, the Foxley dossier did not result in a concrete plan to kill Hitler. Some of the ideas that it contained appeared to be completely bonkers. (Although maybe not as crazy as some of the things Stanley Lovell and the OSS were trying, such as adding female hormones to the Führer's carrots and beets.) And some of these outlandish ideas turned out to be, on further examination, rather interesting.

Among those was the proposal that Rudolf Hess could be hypnotised by the Allies and returned to Germany where he would get close to Nazi leaders and kill them. This idea is similar to the plot of *The Manchurian Candidate*. But in hearing the fictional Red Chinese villain Yen Lo describing how this might work, it was surprising to this writer to discover that the academic papers and the experiments he cited from the early 1940s were *real*. Furthermore, as we now know, the OSS was also considering the use of hypnotised assassins to kill Hitler.

The point is not that hypnotised assassins might have worked. Rather, we have to understand that in 1944–45, there were a number of prominent psychologists making the case, based on their research, that this *could* be done. In addition, there were SOE officers at the highest levels, like Major Manderstam, who had shown an interest in hypnosis. And finally, Rudolf Hess turned out to be *obsessed* with the possibility that hypnosis was being used by the Allies to defeat Germany in the war, and feared it would be used on him.

Conclusion

The American plans to kill Hitler were no more realistic than SOE's, and like the British ones remained largely untested. The Soviets alone seem to have considered practical measures that might have worked, including in 1939, when it would have made a massive difference – only to subsequently see those measures blocked at the highest levels, by Stalin himself.

Timing was central to the story of Operation Foxley. Coming as it did in the final year of the war, it was doomed to remain a brainstorming exercise rather than an operational plan. The exchanges of messages between London and Washington in early 1945, as SOE explored the possibility of using Captain Edmund Bennett as their gunman, seem as divorced from reality as the proposal to hypnotise Hess.

Leading up to and throughout the Second World War, the SOE, as well as the OSS and GRU, looked into ways to kill the German dictator. They considered using a sniper, poisoning Hitler's food and drink, parachuting in teams of commandos to attack his Alpine retreat, sending hypnotically programmed assassins into the Third Reich, or even just blowing him up while he ate lunch at his favourite restaurant in Munich.

Any one of those attempts might have worked. The war would have been shortened and lives saved had such an attempt been made – and had it succeeded. Instead, Hitler was left to spend his final days in a bunker in Berlin, where he eventually took his own life and thus brought an end to the Second World War and the nightmare that was the Third Reich.

APPENDIX

HS 6/624: "Operation FOXLEY"

"HISTORICAL DOCUMENT"
Permanent Preservation

HS6/624

ARCHIVES

| FILE NUMBER S.O.E. GERMANY VOLUME NO. 8. vol. 1. FROM TO | SUBJECT GERMANY - POLITICS OPERATION FOXLEY |

Operation FOXLEY.

TOP SECRET

Contents.

	Pages
INTRODUCTION.	1

PART I - THE BERCHTESGADEN AREA AS THE SCENE OF ACTION.

A. Climate and Topography.

1. Climate.	2
2. General notes on the topography of the area.	2-4
3. Topography of the Obersalzberg.	
(a) General	4-6
(b) Layout of the buildings on the Obersalzberg.	6-34
4. Viewpoints.	34
5. Approaches.	34-42
6. Hideouts in the Berchtesgaden area.	42-43

B. Protection of the Obersalzberg.

1. Security.	
(a) Security personnel.	43-44
(b) Passes.	44-46
2. Troops.	
(a) SS Führerbegleitkommando.	46-48
(b) SS Wachkompanie Obersalzberg.	48-50
(c) SS Sonderkolonne.	48,51
3. Piquets and patrols.	
(a) SS piquets and patrols.	51,52,54,55
(b) Civilian piquets and patrols.	53,55
4. Wire.	53
5. A.A. Protection.	53
6. Air raid precautions	
(a) Warning system.	56
(b) Air raid shelters.	56
(c) Camouflage.	57

	Pages
C. <u>Personalities in the Obersalzberg and their habits</u>	
1. Hitler.	
(a) Appearance.	57-59
(b) Hitler's doubles.	60
(c) Routine at the Berghof.	60-61
2. Other personalities in the Obersalzberg.	62-64
D. <u>Possibilities of action in the Berchtesgaden area.</u>	
1. Timing.	65
2. Suggested course of action	
(a) Action at the Mooslaner Kopf.	65-67
(b) Action on the Berghof-Schloss Klessheim road.	67-69
3. Combined operation.	69

PART II - <u>THE FÜHRERZUG AS THE SCENE OF ACTION.</u>

A. <u>The Führerzug.</u>	
1. General description.	70-71
2. Composition of the Führerzug.	71-78
3. The coaches of the Führerzug.	78-84
(a) A.A. coach.	79
(b) Salonpackwagen.	80
(c) The W/T coach.	81
(d) Secretariatwagen.	82
(e) The dining car.	83
(f) Hitler's Salonwagen.	84
B. <u>Protection of the Führerzug.</u>	
1. Protection on the train itself.	
(a) En route.	85
(b) In the sidings.	85
2. Guarding of the route.	
(a) Stations.	86
(b) Track.	86-87
(c) Warning system.	87-88

	Pages
C. **Servicing of special trains.**	
1. Washing	88
2. Provisioning.	88-89
D. **Routeing of the Führerzug.**	
1. To the north.	89
2. To the west.	90
E. **Possibilities of action in connection with the Führerzug.**	
1. At the Schloss Klessheim sidings.	90-92
2. At Salzburg railway station.	92-95
3. En route.	96-97

APPENDIX I - Hitler's cars.

APPENDIX II - Schloss Klessheim.

APPENDIX III - Foreign workers in Salzburg and district.

APPENDIX IV - Attempt in West Prussia to blow up the Führerzug.

APPENDIX V - "I" as the clandestine means.

Operation.
FOXLEY.

INTRODUCTION.

1. **Object:** The elimination of HITLER and any high-ranking Nazis or members of the Führer's entourage who may be present at the attempt.

2. **Means:** Sniper's rifle, PIAT gun (with graze fuze) or Bazooka, H.E. and splinter grenades; derailment and destruction of the Führerzug by explosives; clandestine means.

3. **Scene of operations:** The most recent information available on Hitler and his movements narrows down the field of endeavour to two loci of action, viz. the BERCHTESGADEN area and the Führerzug (Hitler's train).

    The BERCHTESGADEN area includes the OBERSALZBERG as well as the road from the BERGHOF (Hitler's residence on the OBERSALZBERG) to SCHLOSS KLESSHEIM, one of the alternative Führerhauptquartiers which were set up in Germany following the threat to the RASTENBURG (East Prussia) FHQ by the advance of the Russian armies in Poland.

    Loci of action in connection with the Führerzug include the SCHLOSS KLESSHEIM sidings, SALZBURG railway station and the routes followed by Hitler's train when travelling north (to Berlin) and west (to Mannheim).

4. **Operatives:** Austrian or Bavarian Ps/W with an animus against the Nazis (and Hitler in particular); Poles or Czechs (in view of the large number of foreign workers of these nationalities in the Berchtesgaden – Salzburg district). Operatives might be trained in this country or abroad (e.g. Italy or Slovenia), and dropped over or infiltrated into enemy territory in the vicinity of Salzburg, where if necessary they could make contact with and receive assistance from anti-Nazi friends and relations (Austrians and Bavarians) or from foreign workers (Poles and Czechs).

5. **Planning** Whereas it might be possible to plan and execute the operations described in Part I – Berchtesgaden area – "from the book", a final check-up of conditions in the Salzburg area and/or on the Führerzug's routes would be advised before drawing up the final plan of action. This, it is suggested, should be made on the spot by the operatives (or their leader) entrusted with the execution of the project.

+ Though Hitler, it is quite definite, was there on 3rd August, if not later.

Part I. THE BERCHTESGADEN AREA AS THE SCENE OF ACTION.

A. Climate and Topography.

1. Climate. The climate of BERCHTESGADEN is in general colder in winter and hotter in summer and autumn than in England.

The chief characteristic of the weather is that it is fairly stable. When it rains, it usually goes on for several days or weeks — similarly in the case of snow. There was on one occasion last winter 14 days' downfall of snow. When it is fine it usually stays fine for several days.

Snow falls fairly early because of the altitude, sometimes as early as September. In 1943 snow fell in November, but there was a long spell of fine weather around Christmas.

Fog is very rare, and normally occurs either in the valley, coming no higher than the GUTSHOF, or the heights surrounding the KEHLSTEIN. It is very rare that the BERGHOF and the SS barracks are wrapped in fog. The weather month by month in the period August 1943 - May 1944 was as follows:-

Aug. 1943.	Very fine; rain only on two or three days.
Sept. " .	Very fine and still very warm up to middle of month when it became wet.
Oct. " .	Sky overcast with constant downpours of rain and sleet. Some snow already began to fall.
Nov. " .	Rainy. Occasional snow which did not stay on the ground.
Dec. " .	On 20 Dec. snow began to fall (lasting two weeks). This type of weather went on throughout the winter.
Jan. 1944.	Maximum depth of snow in the OBERSALZBERG was 2 metres — on the ROSSFELD 4 metres and 6-8 metres on the WATZMANN.
Feb. " .	The downfall of snow slackened and by the middle of the month the FUHRERSTRASSE was clear of snow.
March. " .	Still a few days of snow but weather on the whole fine.
April. " .	Occasional snow. Otherwise typical April weather.
May. " .	This type of weather continued into May when it was still possible to ski.

2. General notes on the topography of the area. (see Sketch Map - Fig.1.). OBERSALZBERG lies in an amphitheatre of the Bavarian Alps adjacent to the former Austrian frontier. The dominating peaks and ranges are, in the north-west the UNTERSBERG (1973m.), in the south-west the LATTENGEBIRGE and WATZMANN peaks, in the south the HOHER GOLL (2522m.) and in the east the ROSSFELD ridge (1608m.).

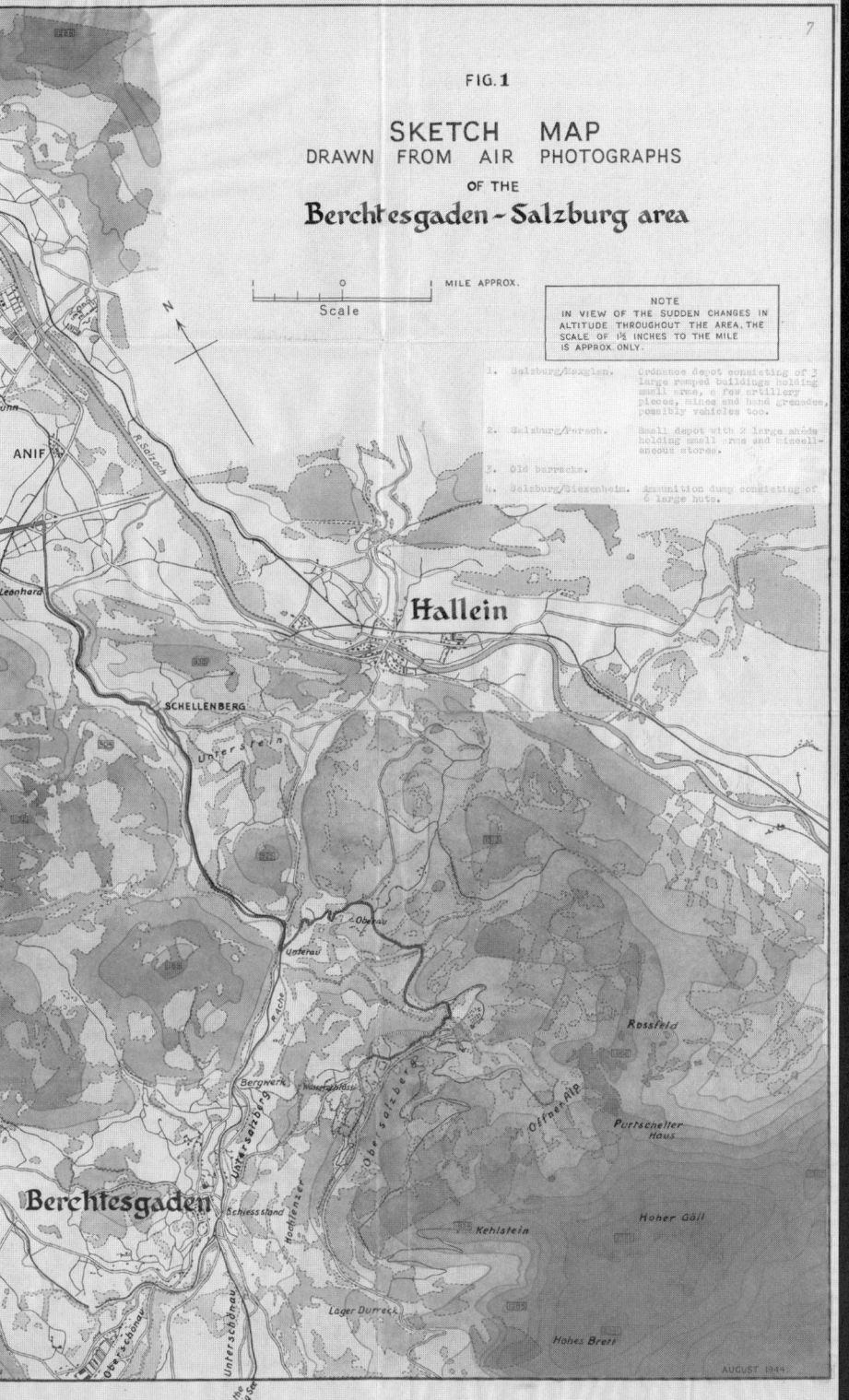

Here the bare limestone peaks and glacier-scaped slopes of the Alps give way to a jumble of pine-clad foothills, interspersed with wide stretches of open grass- and meadowland.

The BAD REICHENHALL-BERCHTESGADEN-HALLEIN area is drained in the east by the SALZACH, in the west by the SAALACH and in the centre by the ACHE which, on leaving the NONNTAL defile (the route taken by HITLER when travelling from the OBERSALZBERG to SCHLOSS KLESSHEIM) enters the SALZBURG plain near St. LEONHARD to flow into the SALZACH south of ANIF.

The greater part of the OBERSALZBERG as well as the road from the BERGHOF as far as GRÖDIG (on the way to SCHLOSS KLESSHEIM) is very hilly and densely wooded and should therefore afford good cover, even in winter, as most of the trees are of the non-deciduous variety.

Since the route taken to SCHLOSS KLESSHEIM makes use of the Autobahn which skirts the MAXGLAN suburb of SALZBURG the attempt would have to be made from the woods between the OBERSALZBERG and GRÖDIG or in the vicinity of the teahouse on the MOOSLANER KOPF.

3. Topography of the OBERSALZBERG (see Fig.2).

(a) General. The entire area of the OBERSALZBERG is for the most part very heavily wooded and, being also extremely hilly, is a difficult area to guard. This is also true of the area immediately around HITLER's residence – the BERGHOF – which is known as the FÜHRERGEBIET. In addition to BORMANN's and GÖRING's residences, the guest houses, the quarters of HITLER's personal and domestic staffs, the SS barracks, the PLATTERHOF – once an hotel-de-luxe and now a hospital – and the hutments of foreign (Czech) workmen, etc., the FÜHRERGEBIET also includes the KEHLSTEIN (or KEHLSTEINGEBIET). The KEHLSTEIN is approached by a zig-zag road (see Fig.1). which however becomes so steep towards the summit that lifts, one for passengers and the other for vehicles, have been installed for the last 300 feet to the Teehouse, a stone building frequently visited by HITLER at one time. Nearby is a wooden hut and in the vicinity a house, hidden away, belonging to BORMANN, in which HITLER is said to have 'lain low' in 1923.

The woods
    in the vicinity of the RODELBAHN;
    behind the MOOSLANER KOPF; (near the Teehaus
        visited by HITLER on his morning walks);
    north of the BERGHOF; and
    round the KEHLSTEIN
are particularly thick.

Except above the 1400 metre line on the KEHLSTEIN, which is a very tricky area to climb, the entire FÜHRERGEBIET is passable on foot. In winter the lower slopes of the KEHLSTEIN are passable on skis, and a very good skier could negotiate the slopes of the RODELBAHN. Skiing on the FÜHRERSTRASSE in the vicinity of the BERGHOF is forbidden.

Fig.2. Key-map of the OBERSALZBERG from air photos.

1. The Berghof.
2. Haus Türken.
3. Gästehaus Hoher Göll.
4. Holtzplatz.
5. Platterhof.
6. Gefolgschaftshaus.
7. SS barracks.
8. Vordereck.
9. Modellbau and Kindergarten.
10. Spahn Häusl.
11. Haus Bormann.
12. Landhaus Göring.
13. Bühnenhöhe.
14. Staatliche Bauleitung.
15. Lager Riemenfeld.
16. Kleushöhe.
17. Hintereck.
18. Adjutantur Göring.
19. Gärtnerei.
20. Post.
21. Kempfhäusl.
22. Jugendverpflegungsheim and Maierhaus.
23. Theaterhalle, Obersalzberg.
24. Lager Antenberg.
25a. Berghäusl.
25b. Haus Speer.
25c. Meisterlehen.
25d. Bergheng.
26. Atelier Speer.
27. Baumgartlehen.
28. Gutshof Obersalzberg.
29. Beckstein Haus.
30. Teehaus (Mooslaner Kopf).
31. Bienenhaus.

——— Tracks.
═══ Roads (vehicles).
▬▬▬ Führerstrasse.
——— Wire fences. (Position of wire fences is only approximate, since they have been sketched from memory).
——— SS patrols.
• SS piquets.
  Civilian piquets, i.e. Posten Berghof, Antenberg, Teugellbrunn, Rosenbahn, Auerstrasse.

Woods (pines and other non-deciduous trees).

Undergrowth, scrub and deciduous trees.

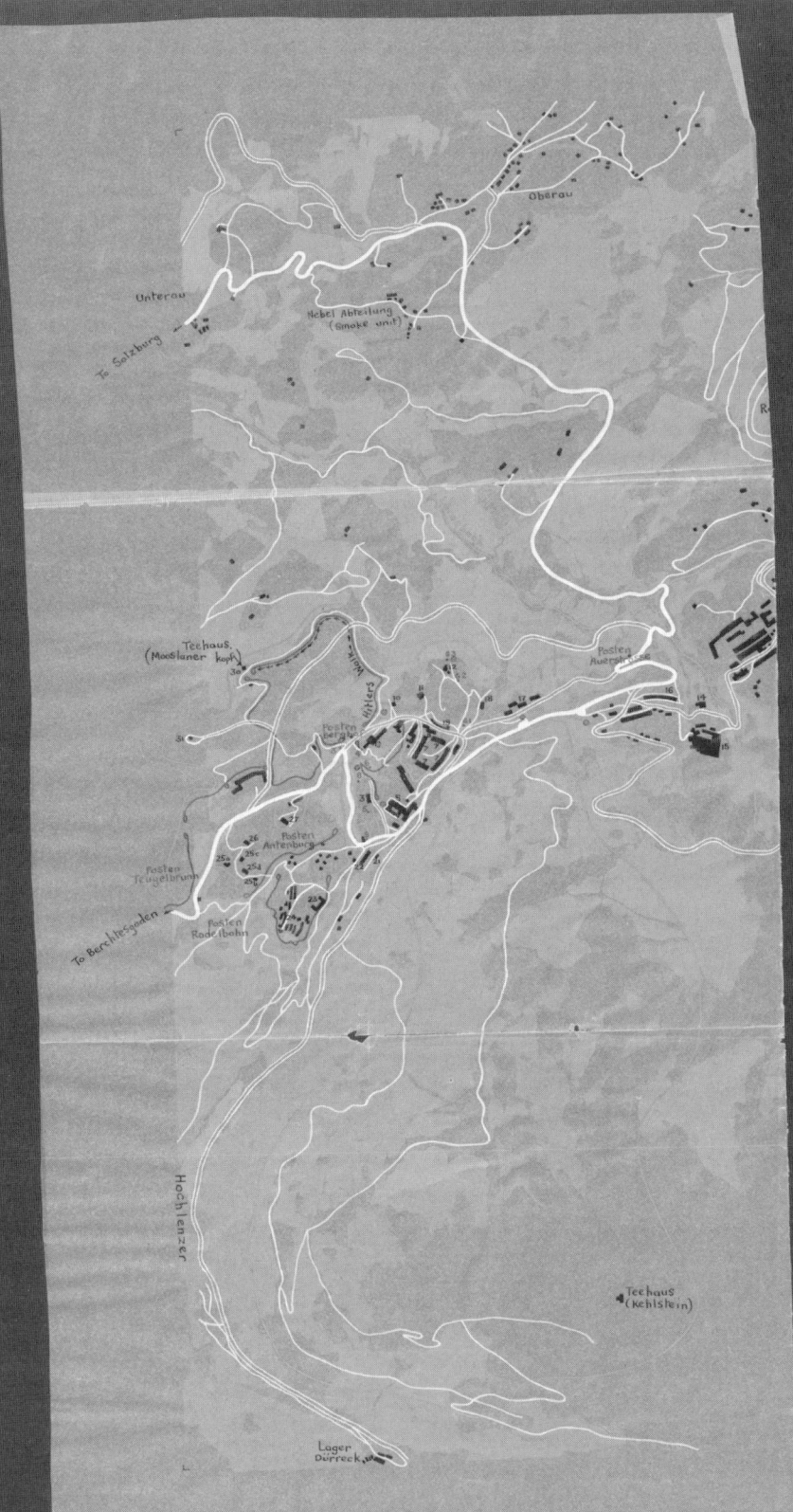

All roads are kept clear of snow in winter. In summer only a few patches of snow remain on the KEHLSTEIN (1834m.).

(b) **Layout of the buildings on the OBERSALZBERG**.
The various buildings in and around the FÜHRERGEBIET are shown in Fig.2. They include:-

(1) **The BERGHOF**. Formerly a chalet with stone ground floor and wooden upper floor known as the HAUS WACHENFELD (Figs.3a-3d), this building has been considerably extended since HITLER acquired it as his country residence in the early 1920s. Figs. 4a, 4b and 5 give an idea of the modifications which have since been made to it. Fig.6 gives a plan of the ground floor of the building (as in April/May 1944). In addition to part of the Begleit-kommando (HITLER's escort) it also houses one of the three telephone exchanges on the OBERSALZBERG.

(2) **HAUS TÜRKEN**. Formerly the Hotel (Pension) ZUM TÜRKEN this building provides sleeping quarters for the piquets of the SS Wachkompanie OBERSALZBERG, the SS guardroom and accommodation for the security personnel (Reichssicherheitsdienst) of the OBERSALZ-BERG. Another telephone exchange is installed here which is operated by personnel of the SS-Kommando OBERSALZBERG. Fig.7 gives plan, side and front elevations of the Haus Türken.

(3) **GÄSTEHAUS HOHER GÖLL**. This guest house lies in the woods back of the BERGHOF in the direction of the KEHLSTEIN. It accommodates Frl. Eva (Evi) BRAUN, Hitler's secretary and Press Chief Dr. DIETRICH on his visits to the BERGHOF as well as Hitler's aides-de-camp and less important guests. It also houses RSD (security) personnel, including Brigadeführer RATTENHUBER, who is in command of the RSD at OBERSALZBERG. The guest house is run by a Frl. JOSEPHA GUGGENBICHLER, who is the "Spiessin" (supervisor) of the women in the district. There is a teleprinter installation in the building which is operated by men of the Führerbegleitbataillon (Hitler's escort battalion) from the Grossdeutschland Division. This unit normally provides the guard at FHQ/OKW. Fig.8 gives plan, side and front elevations of the Gästehaus (see also Fig.11).

(4) **HOLZPLATZ**. This is a sawmill (wooden hut) with a motor-driven saw worked by a German employee who lives on the KLAUSHÖHE.

(5) **PLATTERHOF**. Designed as an hotel-de-luxe and only completed in 1942, the Platterhof (Fig.9) is now a hospital for severely wounded members of the Wehrmacht. It houses some 80-100 patients. The coiffeur in charge of the barber's shop under the hospital (Fig.10) speaks fluent Italian (and German with a Bavarian accent); he employs three Italian assistants.

The Bergschenke (Fig.9) consists of a Bierstube and restaurant with kitchen underneath. Five or six waitresses (wearing blue "Dirndl" dresses) are employed. They live in the GEFOLGSCHAFTHAUS.

Fig. 3a.

Fig. 3b.

Figs. 3a and 3b. Haus Wachenfeld in the 1920s prior to the extensions preceding its transformation into the Berghof. Note: The gateway in Fig. 3a has long since been removed to the Posten Berghof (see Fig.2). The mountain in the background of Fig. 3b is the WATZMANN.

Fig. 3c.

Fig. 3d.

Figs. 3c and 3d showing respectively views of the Haus Wachenfeld from the opposite side to that in Fig. 3b, and of the terrace (Fig. 3d).
Note: The mountains in the background of Fig. 3d are those of the UNTERSBERG (see also view in Fig. 11 taken in the same direction).

Fig. 4a. The Berghof in early summer (Kehlstein in the background).
Note: Servants' quarters (right) and flagpole (left).

Fig. 4b. The Berghof in winter (Kehlstein in the background).

The photograph in Fig. 4b was taken later than that in Fig. 4a and shows telephone exchange extension (left).

Hitler's bedroom is on the first floor (left-hand and centre window).

Fig. 5. The Berghof at a later date. This photograph was taken from more or less the same direction as that in Fig. 3.

Note: Gate is no longer as shown in Fig. 3a (having been removed to Posten Berghof (see Fig. 2).
The extension in the foreground houses the telephone exchange.

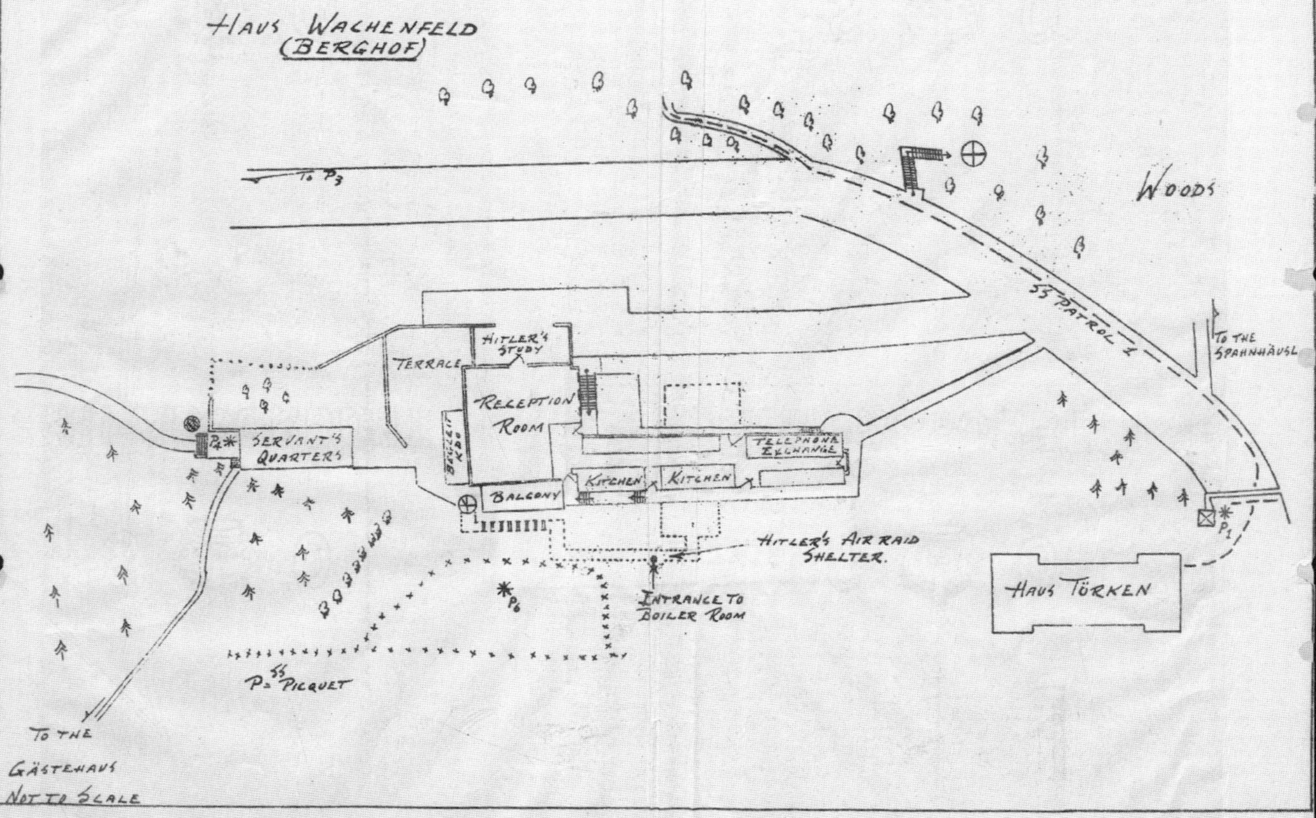

ANNEX 9

HAUS WACHENFELD
(BERGHOF)

WOODS

TO THE SPANNHÄUSL

HAUS TÜRKEN

SS PATROL

TELEPHONE ZENTRALE

HITLER'S AIR RAID SHELTER

KITCHEN

KITCHEN

INMAN'S/ENTRANCE TO BOILER ROOM

HITLER'S STUDY

RECEPTION ROOM

TERRACE

BALCONY

BUFFET ROOM

SERVANT'S QUARTERS

SS PICQUET

TO THE GÄSTEHAUS

NOT TO SCALE

Fig. 6.

ANNEX 8

HAUS TÜRKEN

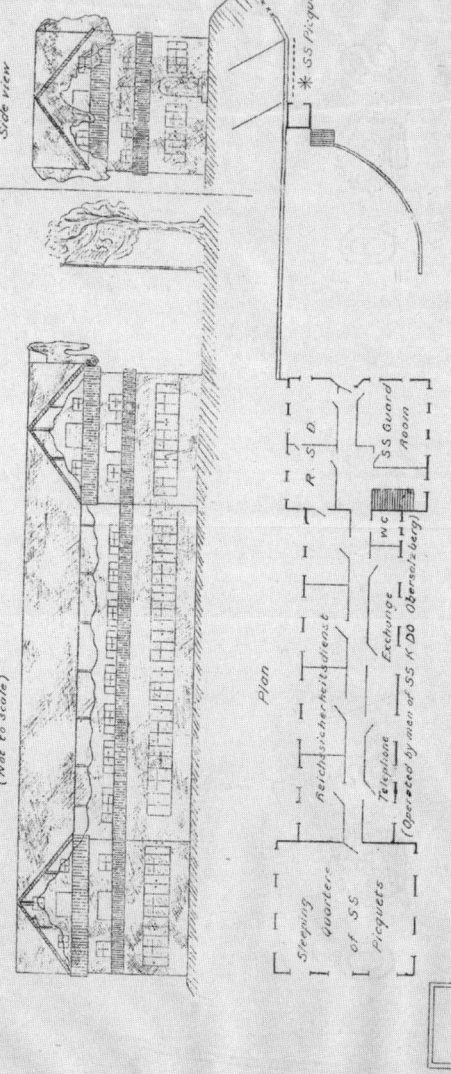

Fig. 7.

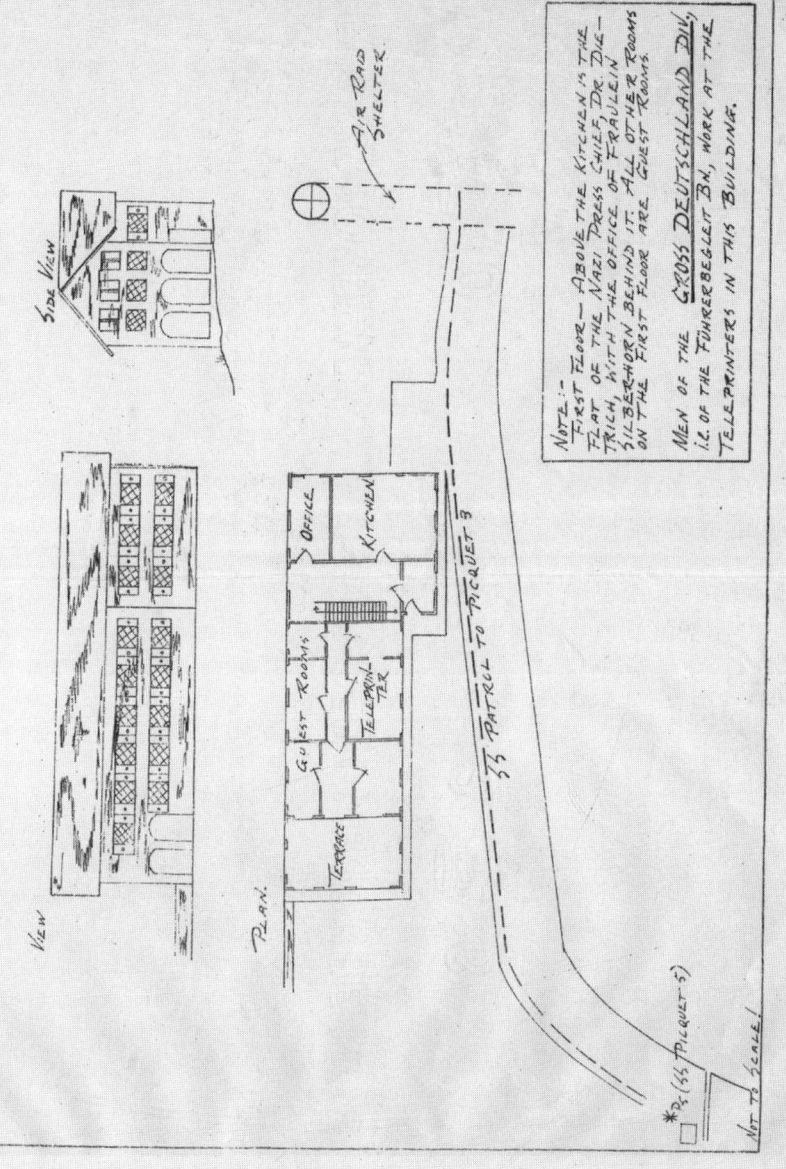

Fig. 8.

-14-

Bergschenke.

DAS SCHÖNE BERGHOTEL

Ein Musterbeispiel für den neuen deutschen Hotelbau: Das Gasthaus „Der Platterhof" auf dem Obersalzberg

Ein Bericht von Ernst Baumann

Das Hauszeichen des neuen Gasthauses

zeigt stilisiert das Bild der Judith Platter, der Heldin des bekannten Romans „Zwei Menschen" von Richard Voß, deren Berghaus früher an dieser Stelle des Obersalzbergs stand.

Inmitten der herrlichen Bergwelt des Berchtesgadener Landes:

Unweit des Berghofs, den sich der Führer erbaute, liegt unmittelbar an der deutschen Alpenstraße eines der schönsten Berghotels des Großdeutschen Reiches, das Gasthaus „Der Platterhof". Von hier aus eröffnet sich die Aussicht auf die gewaltige Runde der Berchtesgadener Felsgipfel. Weit geht der Blick vom Hohen Göll über die Funtensee-Tauern, den Watzmann mit dem Hochkalter, die Reiteralpe und die mächtigen rotbraunen Wände des Untersbergs hinaus zur Feste Hohen-Salzburg und in die weite Ebene. Die Einrichtung des Hauses kann als Vorbild deutscher Wohnkultur gelten.

*

Platterhof.   Post Office.

Gästehaus, Hoher Göll.

Fig.9. Platterhof (exterior).

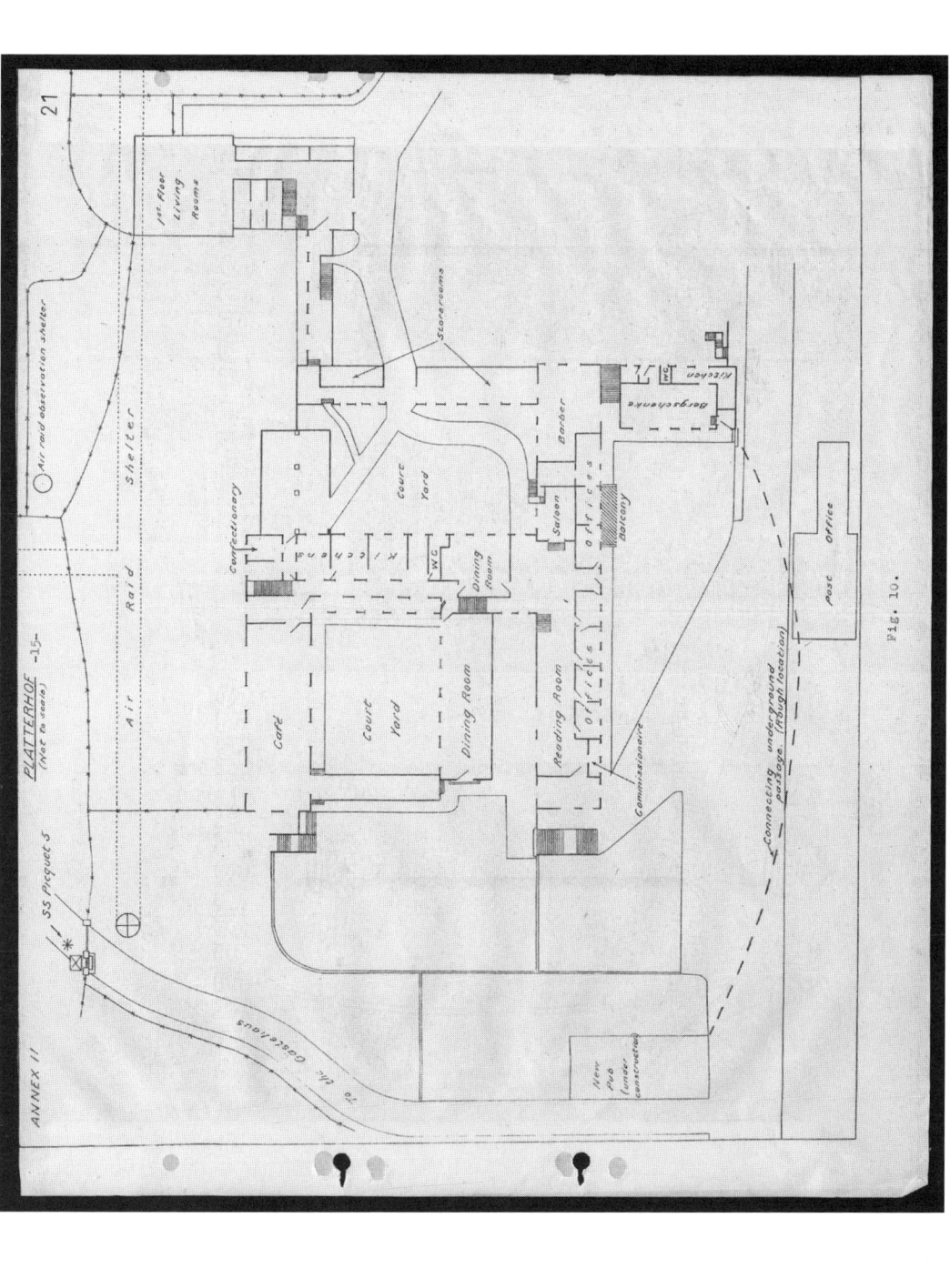

Fig. 10.

The Cafesaal (Fig.10) was, in April 1944, open to the public. There are 5 or 6 waitresses there and 3 or 4 foreign (French) waiters. Fig.11 shows the interior of the Platterhof hotel as it still was in 1944, when it was being used as a hospital.

(6) **The GEFOLGSCHAFTHAUS**. provides accommodation for the nurses and staff of the PLATTERHOF; the porters, clerks, etc. live at the back. There is a garage under the building for two buses (Fig.9) which take the patients in the hospital to the theatre in SALZBURG, etc.

(7) **SS Barracks**. The general layout of the SS barracks is shown in the sketch in Fig.12. Detailed plans, side and end elevations of the buildings, including garages and gymnasium are given in Figs.13-16. In addition to housing the SS Wachkompanie, it includes the offices of the SS-Kommando OBERSALZBERG and of the STOLLENBAUKOMPANIE (Air Raid Shelter Construction Co.).

(8) **VORDEREOK**. (Fig.17). This consists of two houses. The first houses the Verwaltung OBERSALZBERG (Administrative Headquarters of the District) on the ground floor, with servants' quarters on the upper floor. Members of the Begleitkommando sleep here when HITLER is at the BERGHOF. The second house contains the LUFTSCHUTZBEFEHLSTELLE (air raid control room) which is under the direction of Untersturmführer BREDOW.

(9) **MODELLBAU and KINDERGARTEN**. (Fig.18). The MODELLBAU, being built into the rock, is thought to be safer than many of the other buildings and on this account is used by BORMANN as a store for his carpets. It takes its name from the model it contains of the OBERSALZBERG district.

The KINDERGARTEN takes about 20-30 children belonging to the families of officials living in the neighbourhood; BORMANN's children attend.

(10) **SPAHN HAUSL**. The house of Sturmbannführer SPAHN, who is in charge of the SS Administration of OBERSALZBERG, and his wife.

(11) **HAUS BORMANN**. The residence of the BORMANN family, consisting of BORMANN, his wife and his 9-11 children.

(12) **LANDHAUS GÖRING**. (Fig.19). The residence of the GÖRING family i.e. Hermann, Emma and the little Edda. The house is run by the ZICZKA family.

(13) **BÜCHENHÖHE**. A large settlement for children evacuated from bombed cities. It includes a fire station with quarters for fire chief Oberscharführer WAGNER, his wife and mother.

(14) **STAATLICHE BAULEITUNG**. Bureau and garage of the State Office of Works.

(15) **LAGER RIEMNFELD**. Hutments housing Czech workmen (administrative officials are German).

-17-

Eines der hundert Gastzimmer des Platterhofer.
Aus dem Fenster geht der Blick auf den Untersberg.

Im großen Speisesaal des Hauses.
Marmorsäulen tragen die holzgetäfelte Decke.

In der Empfangshalle.
Die Verwendung edler heimischer Werkstoffe und ihre sorgfältige Abstimmung aufeinander erzielen eine Wirkung, die dem Stil und der Zweckbestimmung des Hauses aufs beste entspricht. Die Einrichtung stammt von dem Münchener Innenarchitekten Professor Heinrich Michaelis.

Die Frühstücksstuben sind besonders gemütlich.
Ihre Wände und Decken sind mit dem astreinen Holz der Bergkiefer getäfelt.

Am Abend in der Bibliothek.
Beim Bau des Gasthauses wurden alle Mittel neuzeitlicher Hoteltechnik benutzt. Durch die hervorragende Einrichtung und die herrliche Lage entstand hier ein vorbildliches Berg-Gasthaus.

Fig.11. Platterhof (interior).

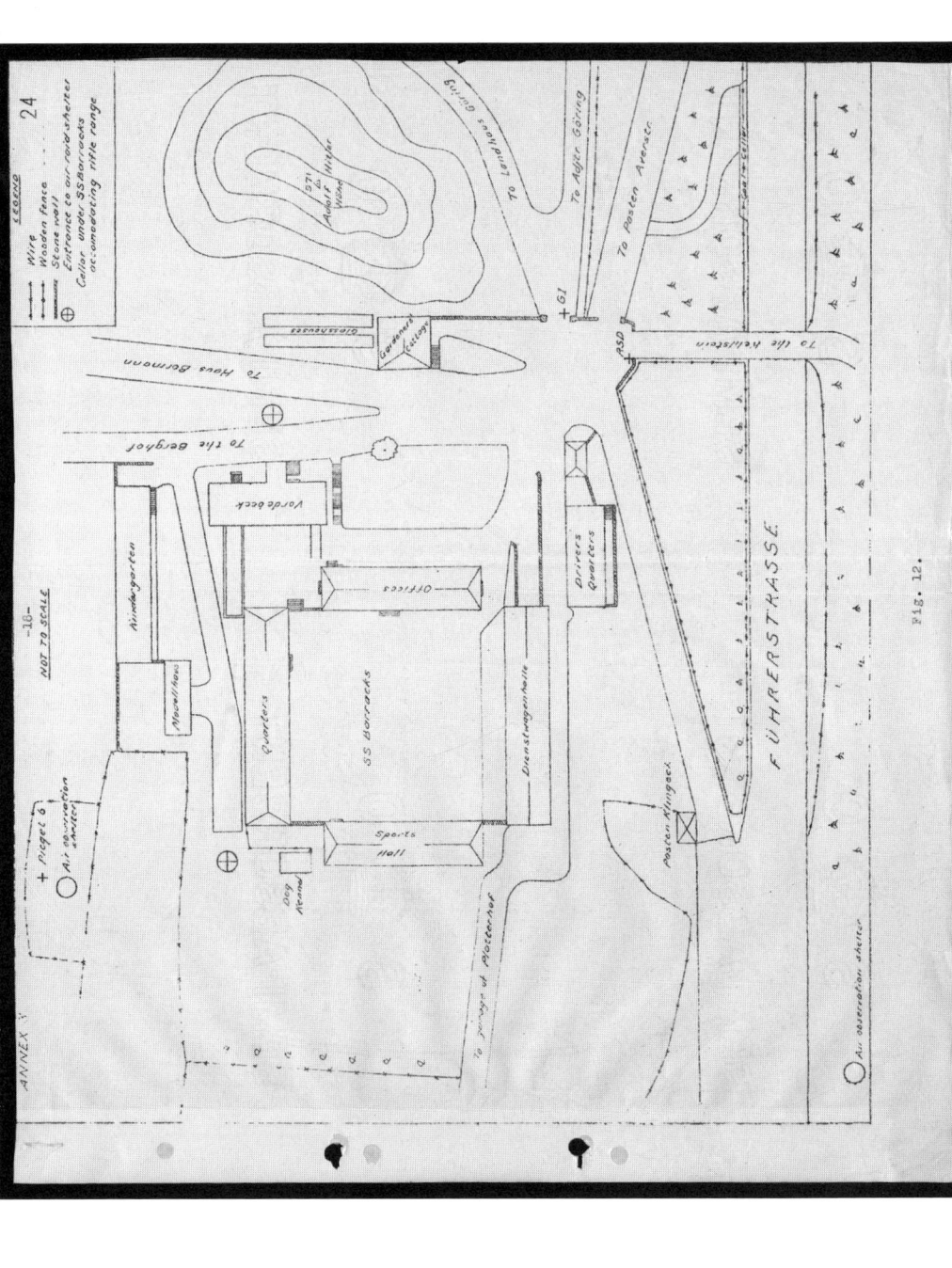

Fig. 12.

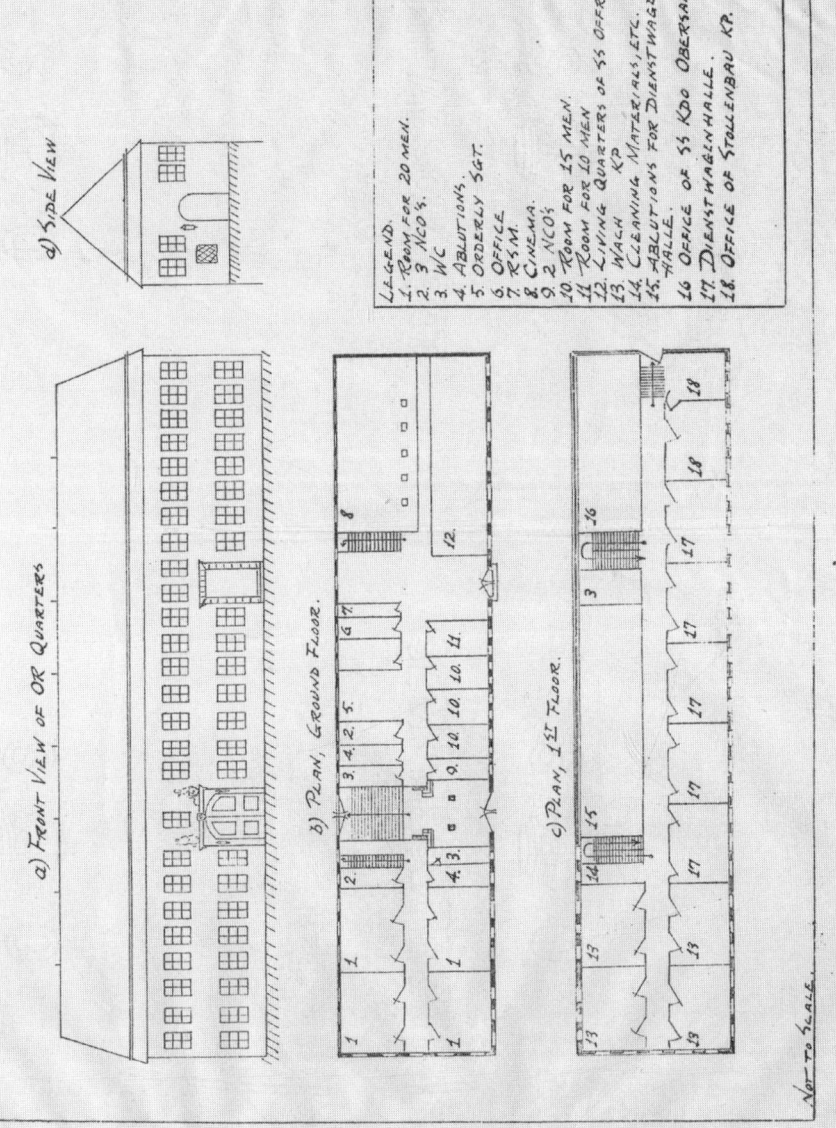

ANNEX 4. SS BARRACKS, OBERSALZBERG.

Fig. 13.

Annex 5

S. S. BARRACKS.

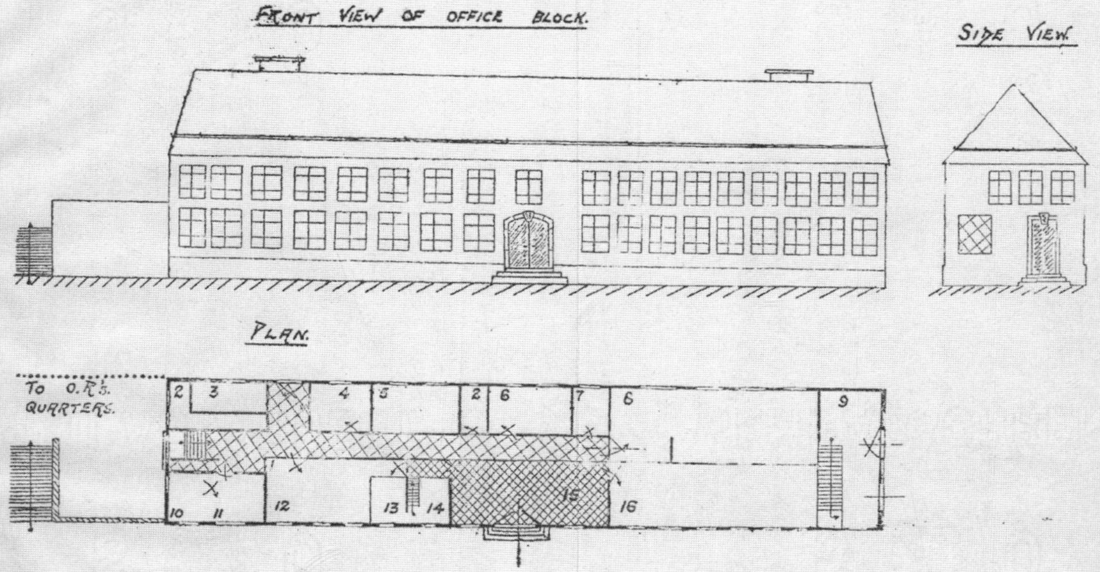
FRONT VIEW OF OFFICE BLOCK.
SIDE VIEW.
PLAN.
TO O.R'S. QUARTERS.
2
3
4
5
2
6
7
6
9
1
10
11
12
13
14
15
16

LEGEND:
1. PUBLIC TELEPHONE.
2. W.C.
3. OFFICE
4. FRL. ANGERER.
5. DINING ROOM FOR FEMALE STAFF.
6. PANTRY.
7. OSCHA TAPPE.
8. KITCHEN.
9. SICK BAY.
10. OSCHA JÄGER.
11. STUBAF SPAHN.
12. CANTEEN
13. TAPROOM.
14. WINE CELLAR.
15. CORRIDOR.
16. O.R'S DINING ROOM.

Fig. 14.

ANNEX 6.

S.S. BARRACKS.

FRONT VIEW OF THE DIENSTWAGENHALLE.

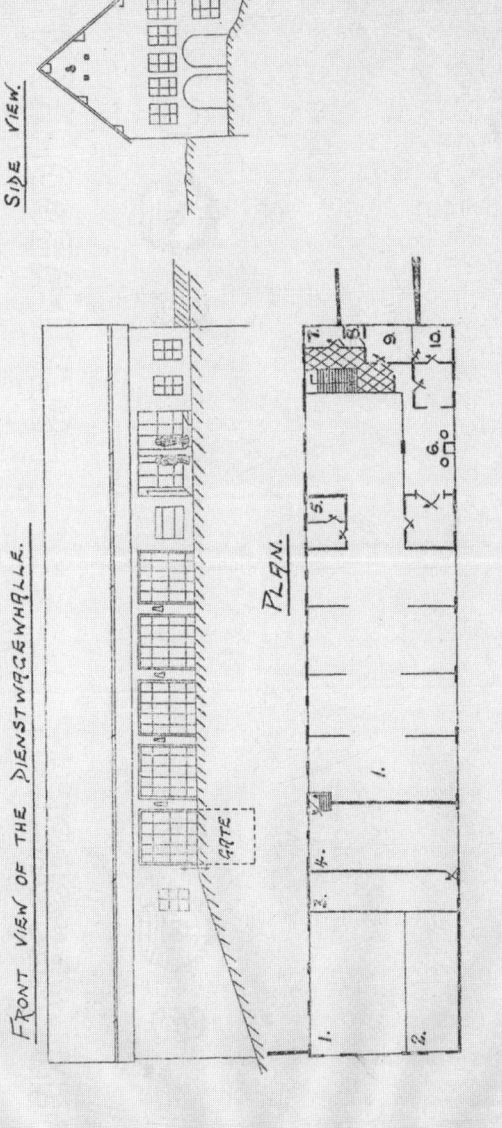

PLAN.

SIDE VIEW.

LEGEND.
1. GARAGES.
2. SPARE PARTS.
3. FIRE HOSES.
4. FIRE FIGHTING EQUIPMENT.
5. M.T. STT.
6. PETROL PUMPS.
7. W.C.
8. HAUPTSCH. REERL.
9. DRIVERS STANDING BY.
10. OSTUF. KREIP.

Fig. 15.

ANNEX 7. S.S. BARRACKS.

-22-

(e) FRONT VIEW OF GYMNASIUM AND WALL CONNECTING IT WITH O.R. QUARTERS.

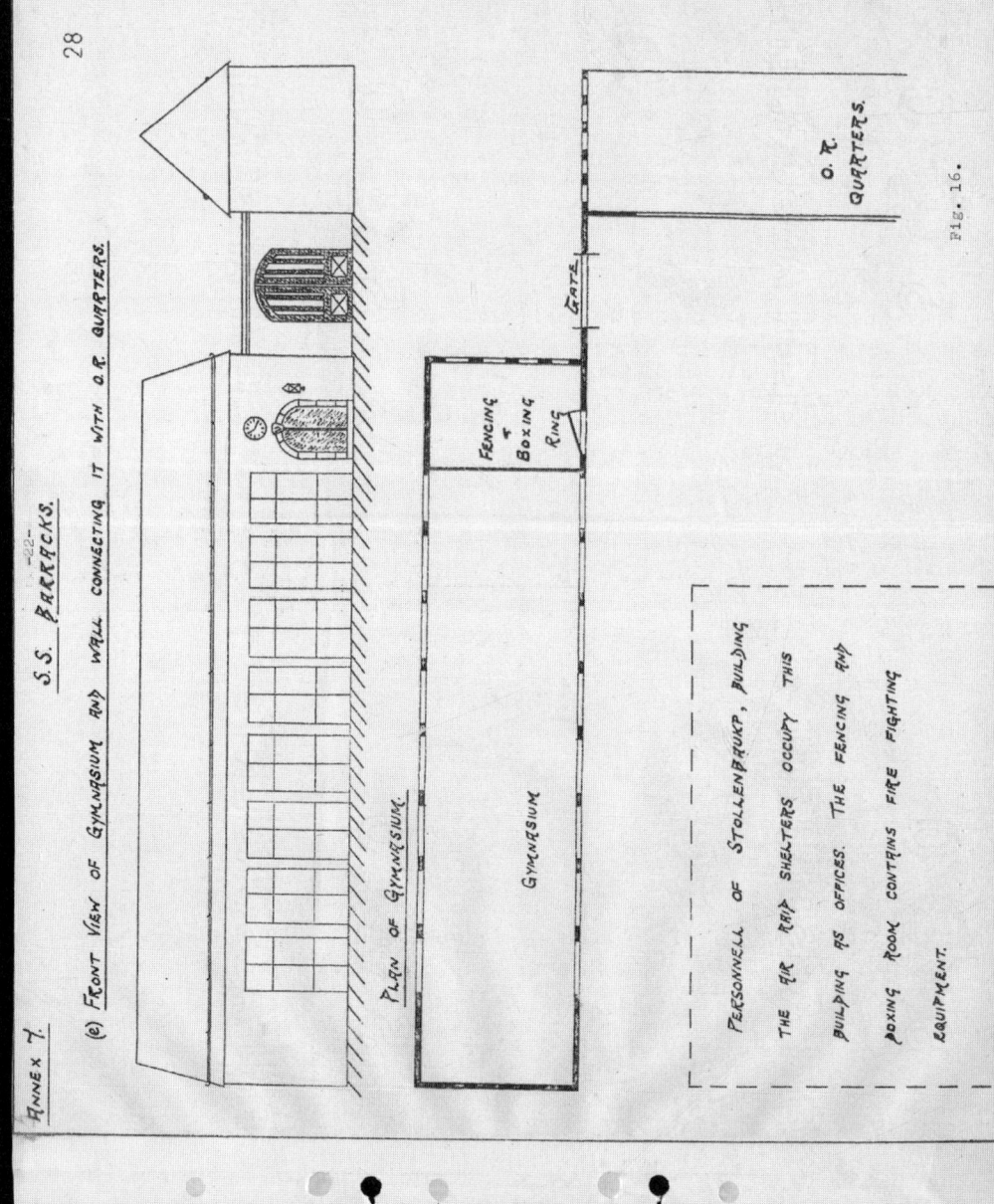

Fig. 16.

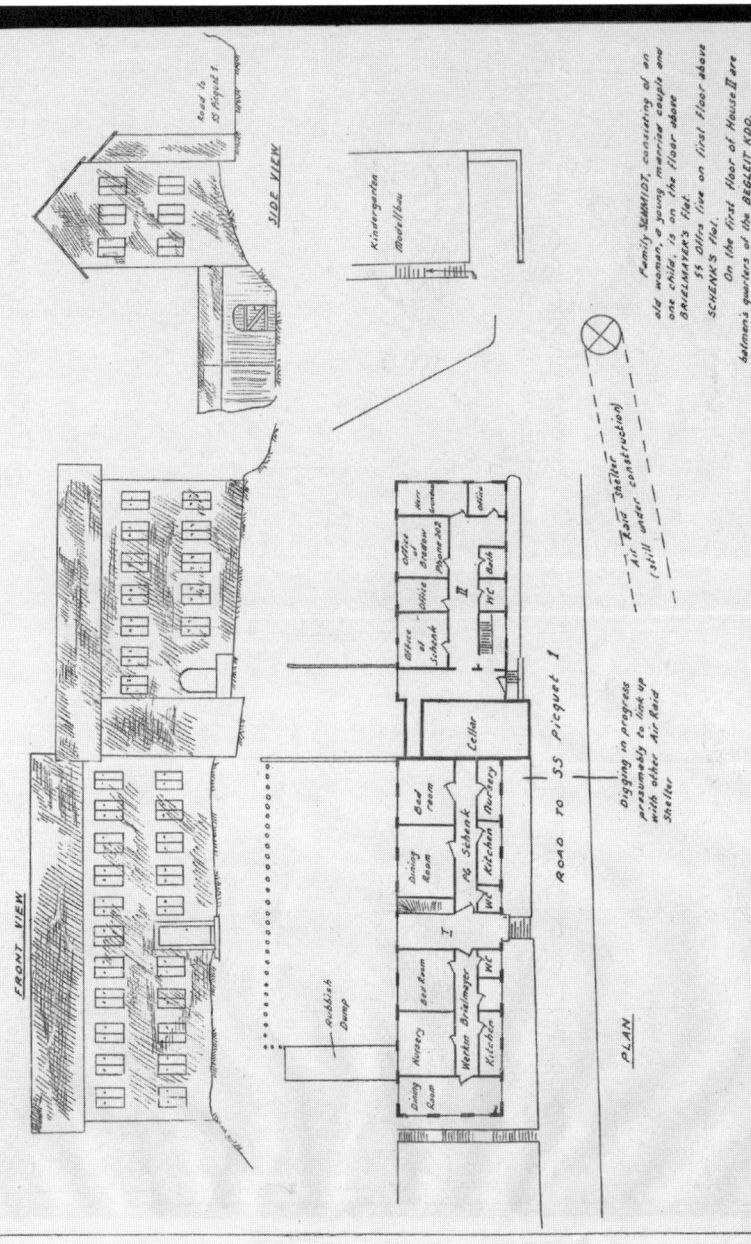

Fig. 17.

ANNEX 25: KINDERGARTEN AND MODELLBAU

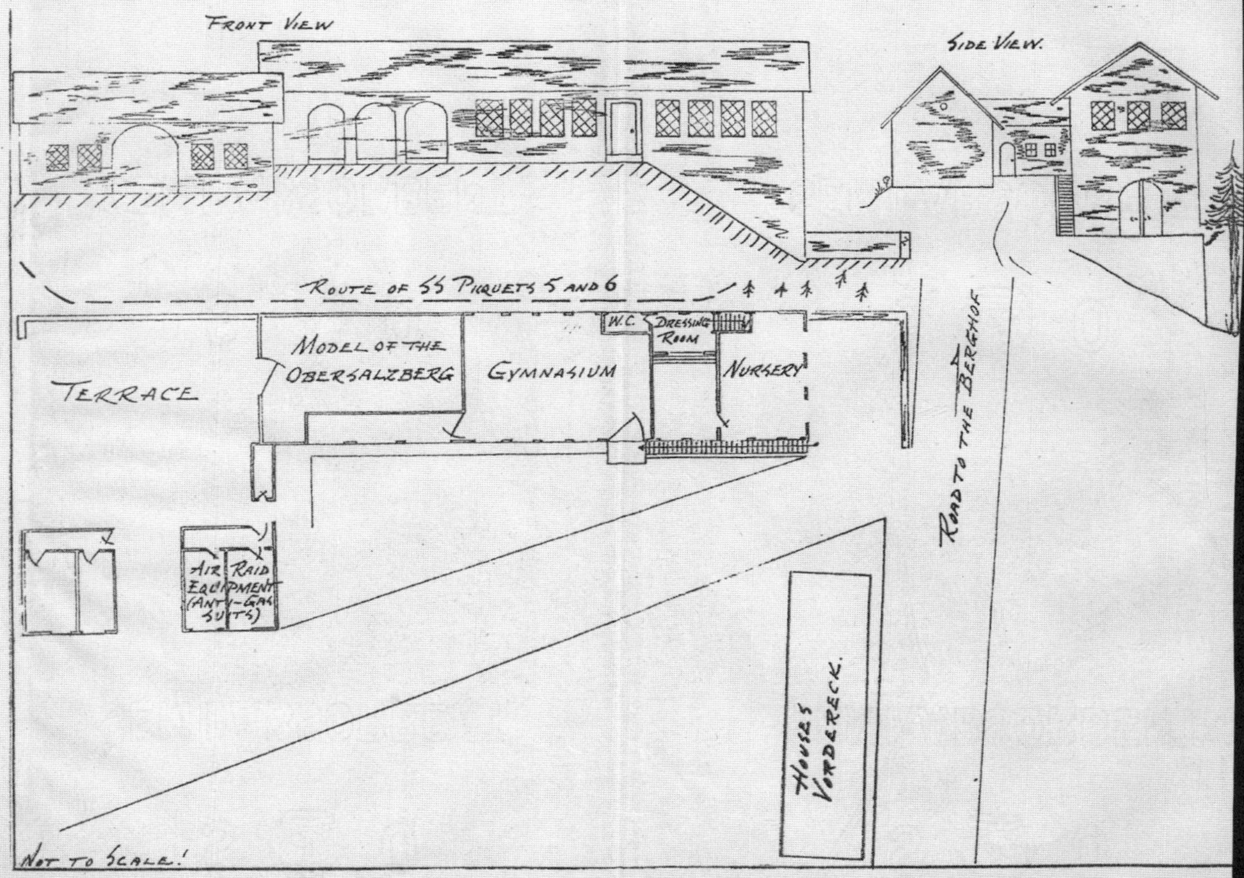

FRONT VIEW

SIDE VIEW

ROUTE OF SS PIQUETS 5 AND 6

W.C. / DRESSING ROOM / NURSERY

MODEL OF THE OBERSALZBERG

GYMNASIUM

TERRACE

AIR RAID EQUIPMENT (ANTI-GAS SUITS)

ROAD TO THE BERGHOF

HOUSES VORDERECK.

NOT TO SCALE!

Fig. 18.

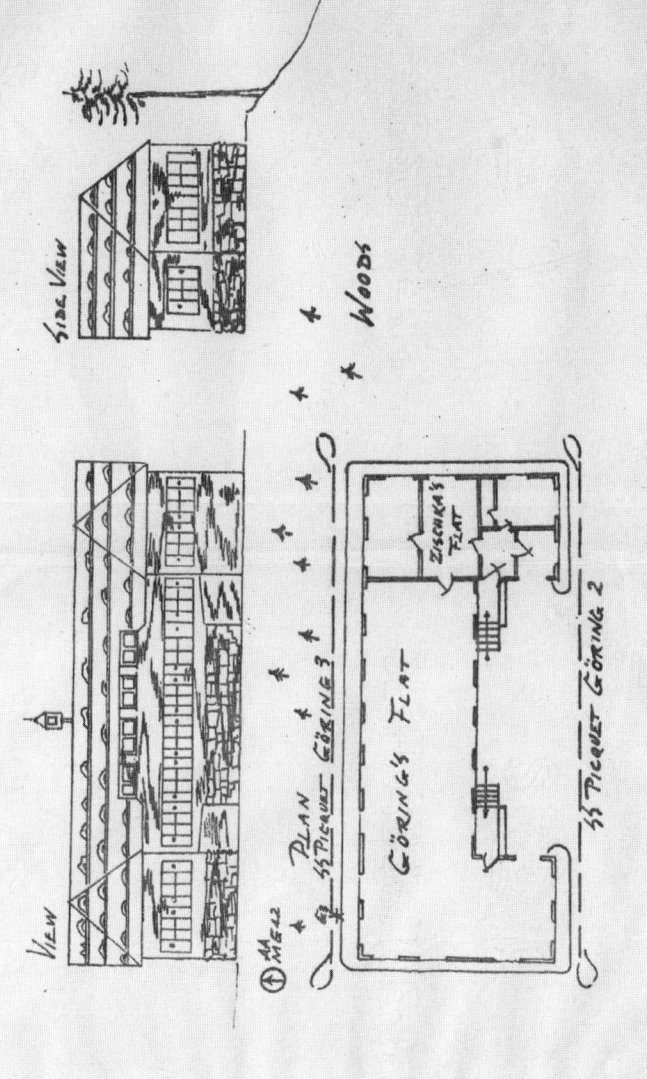

(16) KLAUSHÖHE. This Arbeitersiedlung (workers' settlement) consists of three rows of houses inhabited by German workmen.

    1st. row(1-6) : House 1 - Grocery shop
                            (kept by ZÖLLNER)
                Houses 2-5 - Civilians
                House 6 - Women working in
                          the SS barracks.

    2nd. row(7-14): German workmen

    3rd. row(15-22):House 18 - doctor (an SS
                            Hauptsturmführer)
                  House 22 - Herr GRÜNDMER i/c
                            rations at SS barracks.

(17) HINTERECK (Figs.20a and 20b). This consists of 3-4 houses for the accommodation of officials, including Untersturmführer BREDOW.

(18) ADJUTANTUR GÖRING (Fig.21). This building accommodates Göring's staff (when Göring is at the OBERSALZBERG) and General der Flieger BODENSCHATZ, GAF liaison officer at FHQ. It also contains one of the three telephone exchanges on the OBERSALZBERG.

(19) GÄRTNEREI includes glasshouses for providing vegetables and fruit for the SS in the barracks, and gardener's cottage (see Fig.38).

(20) POST (Fig.22). The Post Office is run by a Party member (who wears the gold Party badge) with three girl assistants, one clerk and a postman who lost an arm in the last war.

Above the Post Office is a shop which sells souvenirs (probably connected with the Platterhof which is opposite - see Fig.11).

(21) KAMPFHÄUSL (Fig.23). It was here that HITLER completed "Mein Kampf". Empty in April/May 1944. The footpath to the Platterhof is public.

(22) JUGENDVERPFLEGUNGSHEIM (Fig. 24) and the MAIERHAUS. The former was empty in April 1944; the latter accommodated the FORZ family of which the daughter is employed at the Post Office.

(23) THEATERHALLE OBERSALZBERG (Fig.25). A wooden structure with gabled roof which collapsed under the weight of snow in the winter of 1943/44. Its reconstruction was scheduled for August 1944. It seats 2000. The flat back of the stage is occupied by Party member FILLHUBER.

Shows are given at 2000 hours on Tuesdays, Thursdays and Saturdays; there is a matinee on Saturdays at 1500 hours. Meetings are also held there. Attendance is compulsory for the SS Wachkompanie.

(24) LAGER ANTENBERG. This camp houses the employees of the Bauleitung OBERSALZBERG Arge and the Bauleitung HOLZMANN & FRANKE. The employees are mostly Czechs chiefly employed on road repairs and improvements, and, in winter, clearing the roads

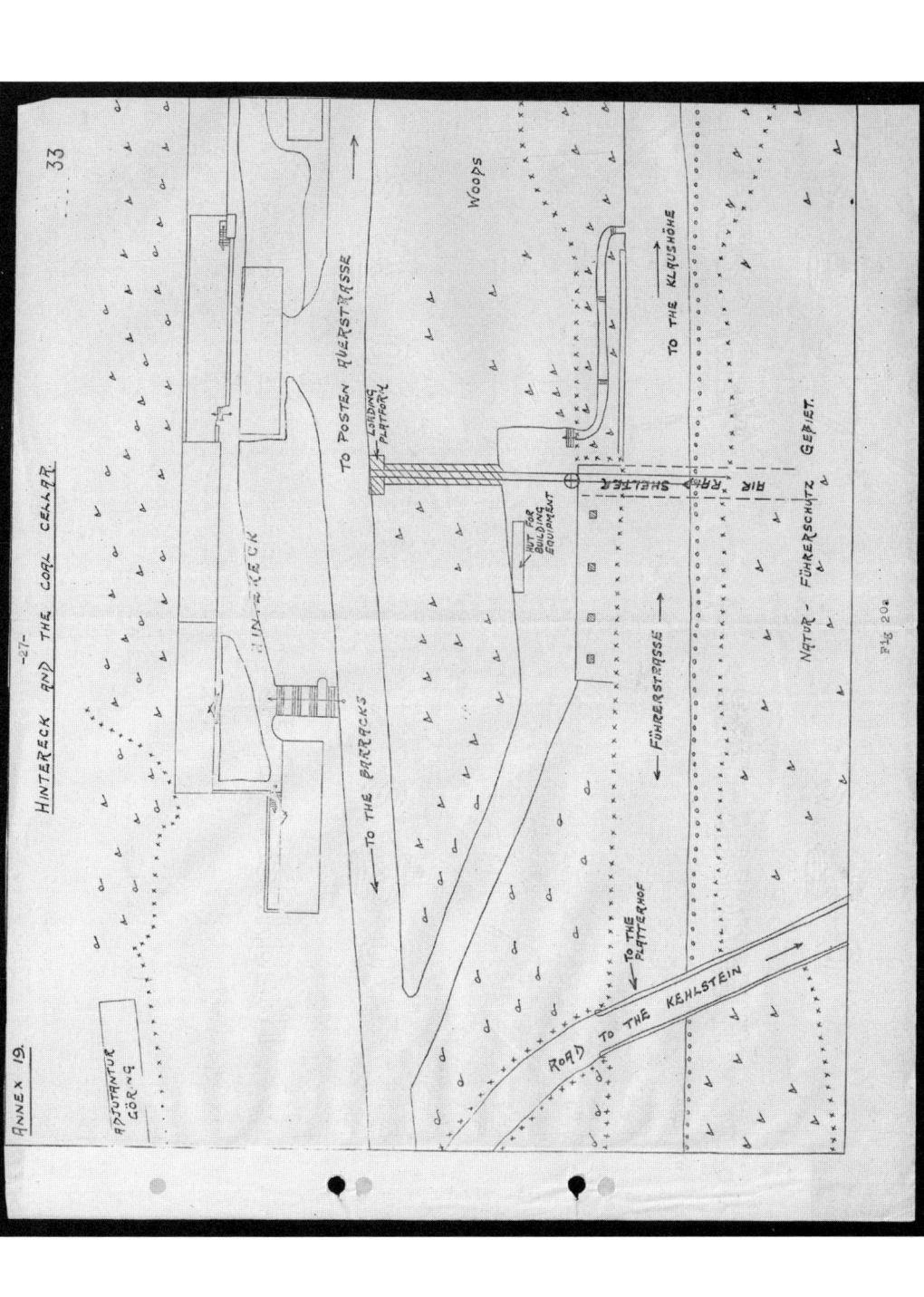

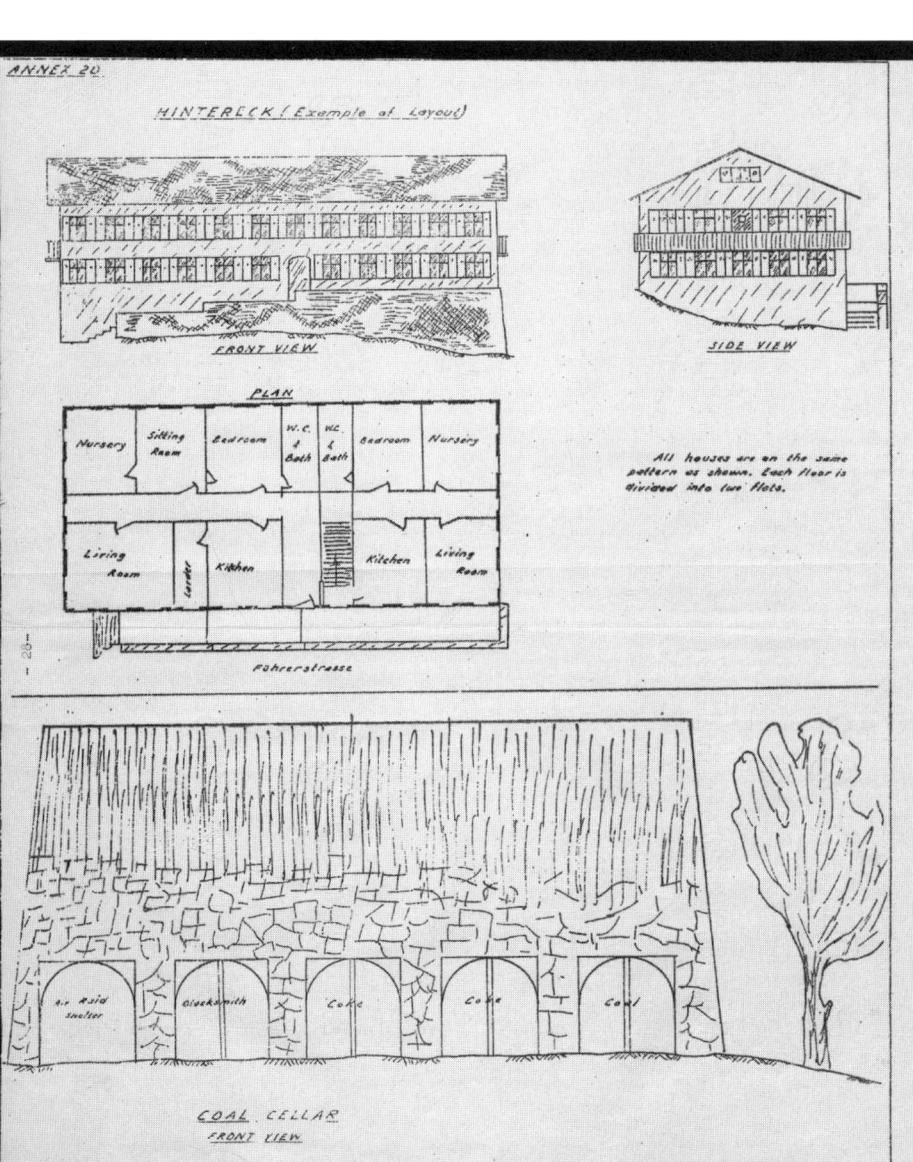

ADJUTANTUR GÖRING -21-   35

FRONT VIEW

SIDE VIEW

Road

Road

To Göring's House

Not to Scale

NOTE:—
THE HOUSEKEEPER'S FLAT IS IN THE CELLAR, WHERE THE TELEPHONE EXCHANGE IS PROBABLY LOCATED.

THERE IS A WIRELESS STATION UNDER HAUS BORMANN FOR USE IN EMERGENCIES.

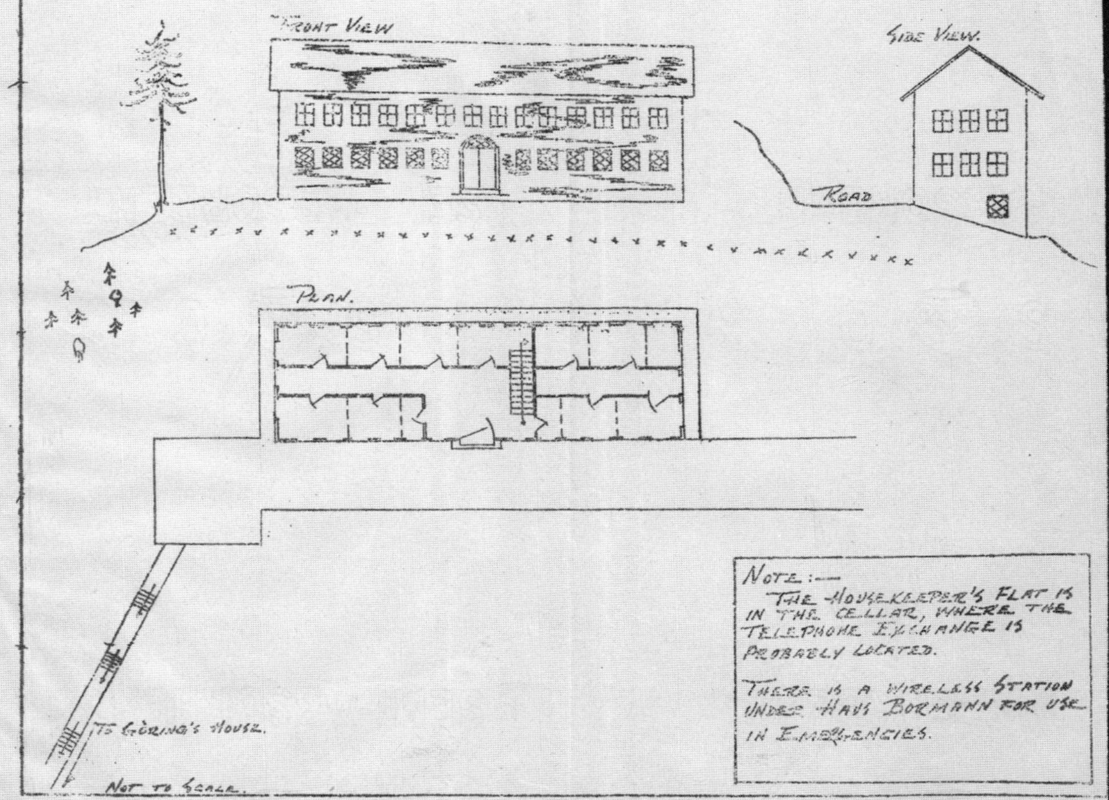

Fig. 21.

ANNEX 27

- 30 -

POST OFFICE OBERSALZBERG

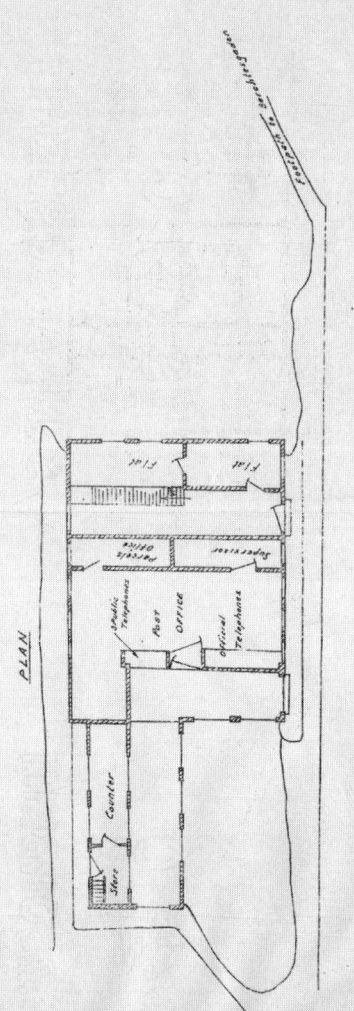

Fig. 22.

Not to Scale

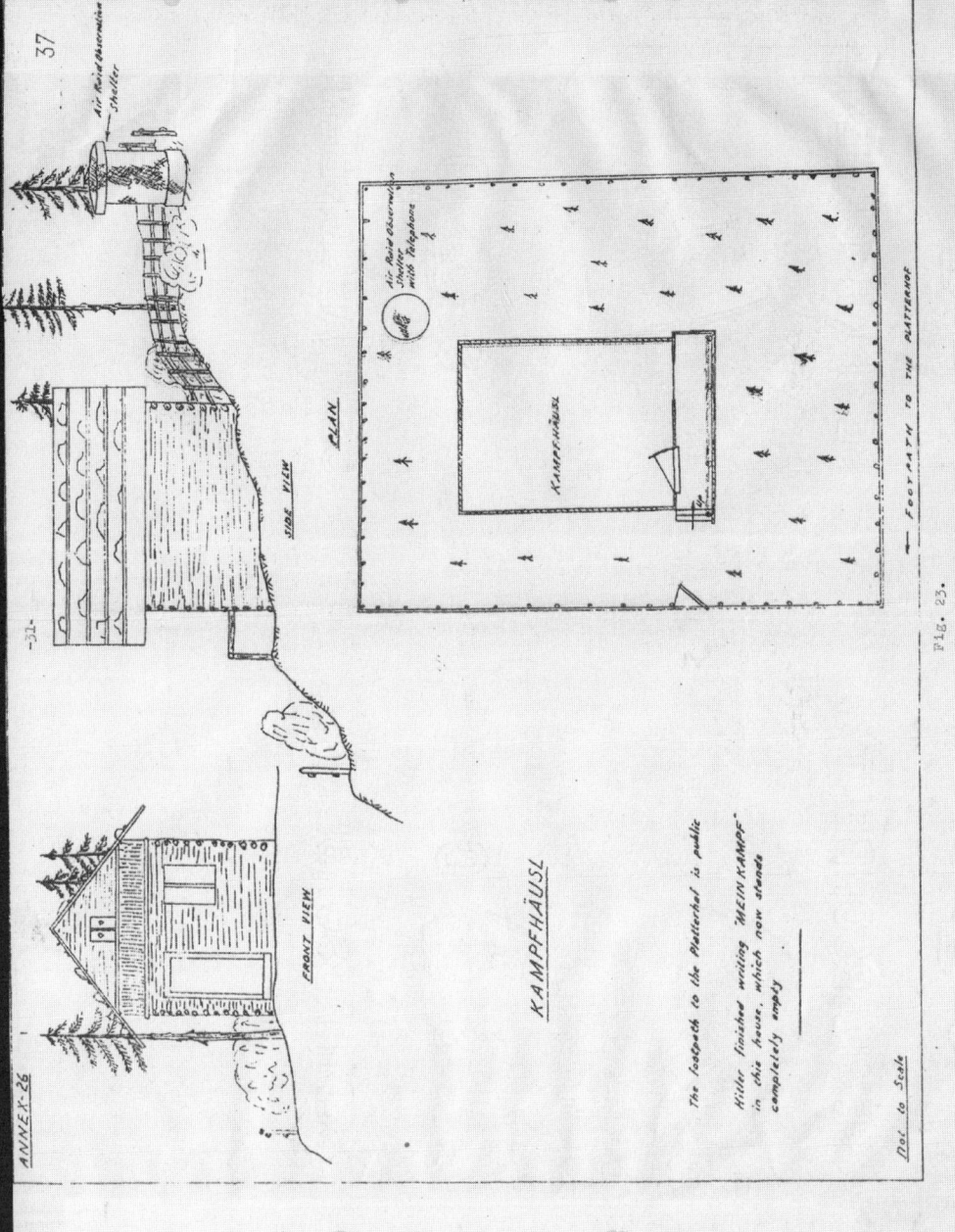

KAMPFHÄUSL

The footpath to the Platterhof is public.

Hitler finished writing "MEIN KAMPF" in this house, which now stands completely empty.

Fig. 23.

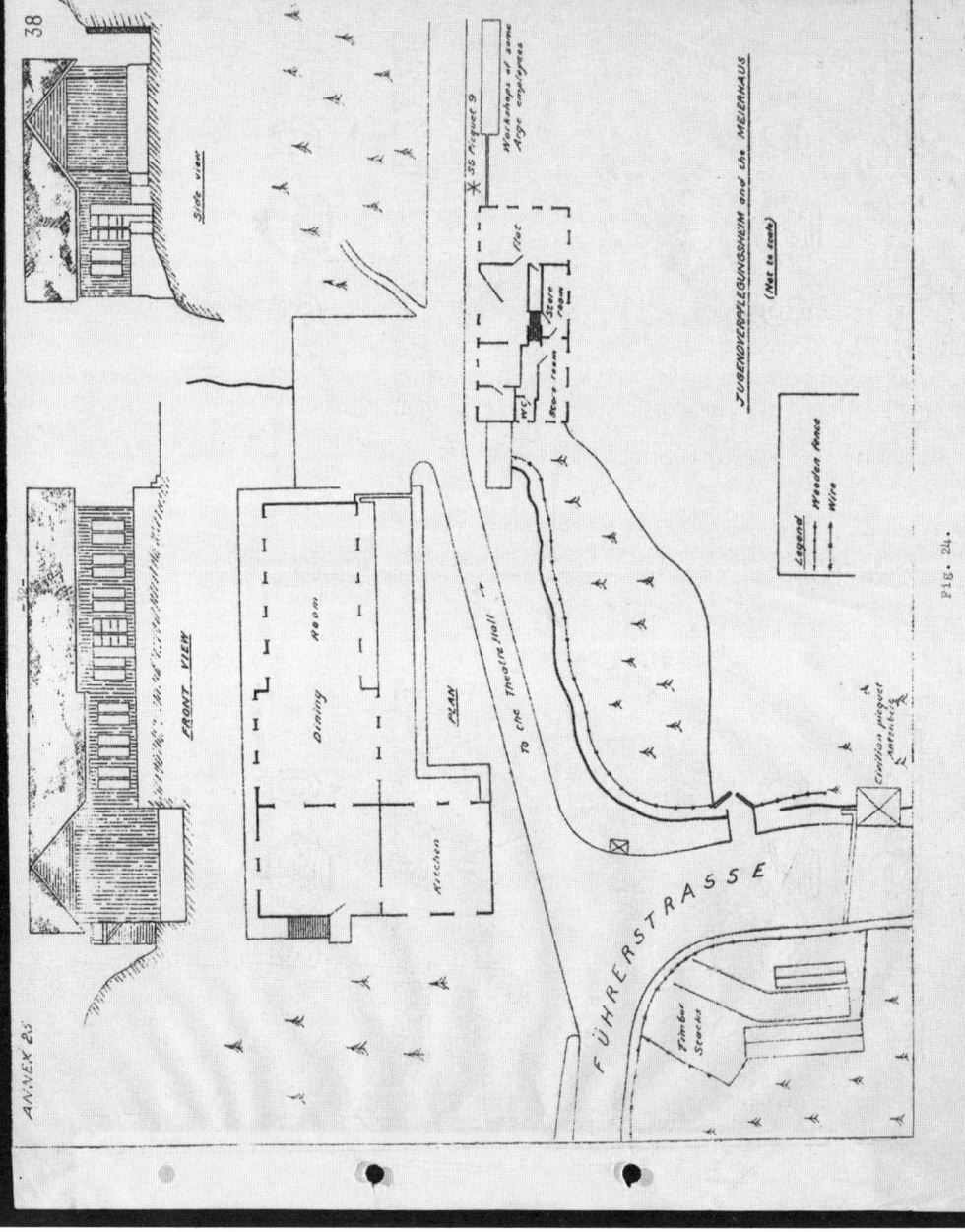

Fig. 24.

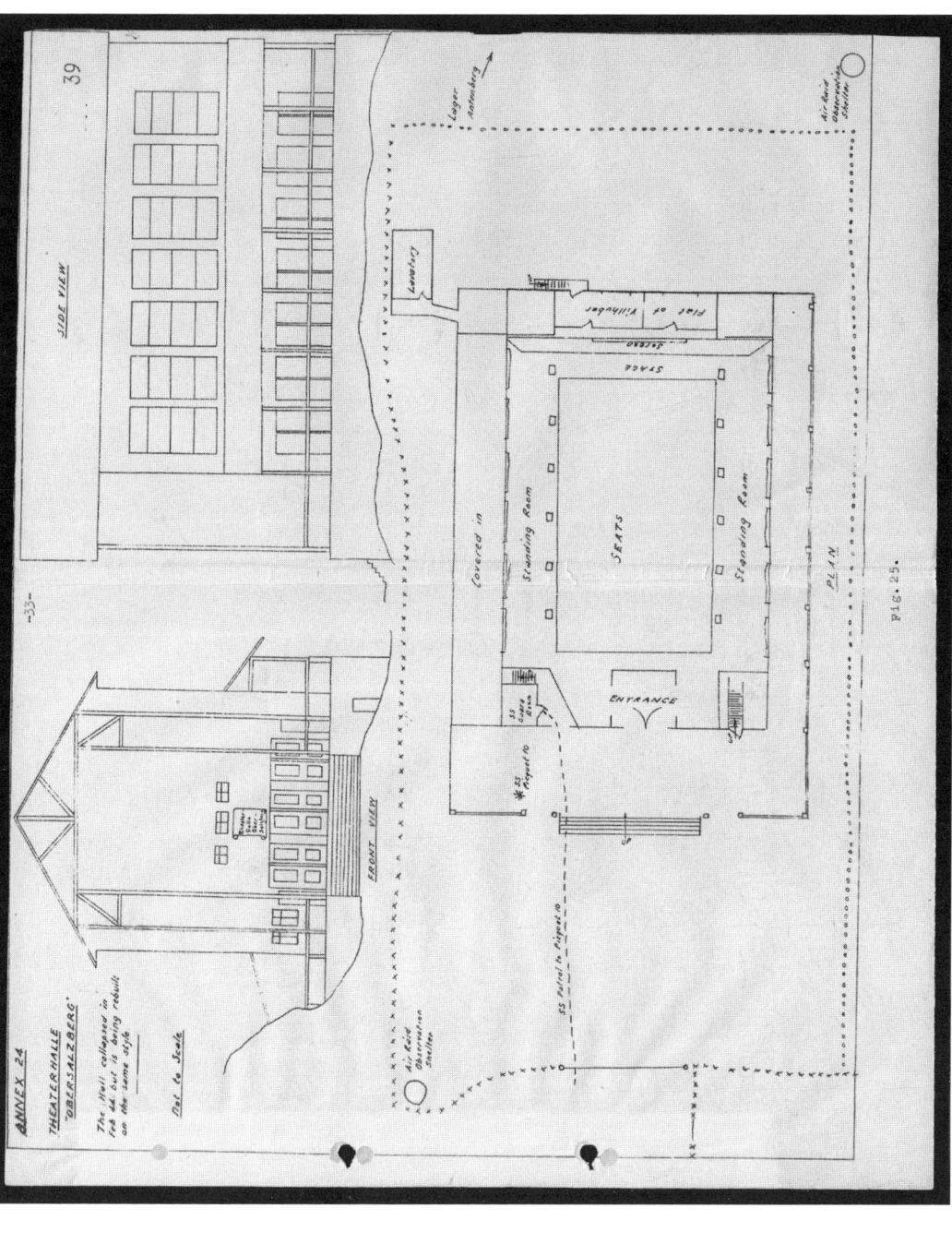

of snow. Behind the camp is a dump of timber for constructional purposes and a wooden shed.

(25) BERGHAUSL, HAUS SPEER, MEISTERLEHEN and BERGHANG (Fig.26). The BERGHAUSL and the BERGHANG house civilians. HAUS SPEER is the residence of the SPEER family (wife, children and nurse of Reichminister SPEER). The MEISTERLEHEN is a dilapidated house and is unoccupied.

(26) ATELIER SPEER (Fig.27) is now used to accommodate children from bomb-damaged areas. It takes about 40 children.

(27) BAUMGARTLEHEN (Fig.28). This is the chief pigsty (Schweinstelle) of the GUTSHOF. It includes living quarters for the swineherds.

(28) GUTSHOF OBERSALZBERG (Fig.29). This, the home farm of the BERGHOF, supplies the latter with milk and butter, etc.

(29) BECHSTEIN HAUS (formerly the HESS HAUS) is now a guest house for HITLER's more important guests, e.g. the late King Boris. MUSSOLINI usually stops there when he visits the BERGHOF. It is kept by an SS Oberscharführer and his wife.

(30) TEEHAUS (MOOSLANER KOPF) is in use— unlike the Teehaus on the KEHLSTEIN which was empty in April/May 1944. It is used by HITLER as the objective of his morning walks, now that he appears no longer to visit the KEHLSTEIN.

(31) BIENENHAUS. This is the apiary belonging to the GUTSHOF.

4. Viewpoints.

The entire Führergebiet can be seen from the KEHLSTEIN, the HOHER GOLL, the HOHES BRETT and the WATZMANN.

The BERGHOF is visible from the SCHELLENBERG-UNTERAU road and from the Cafe Rottenhöfer in BERCHTESGADEN. The DOKTORBERG near BERCHTESGADEN also commands a good view of most of the area.

A panorama of the area, taken from near BERCHTESGADEN, is shown in Fig.30.

The teahouse on the MOOSLANER KOPF is visible from the BERCHTESGADEN-UNTERAU road. The Landhaus GÖRING can be seen from OBERAU.

5. Approaches.

(1) Leave BAD REICHENHALL via the PREDIGSTUHL Bahn (Fig.31) at the top of which is a hospital, formerly an hotel (Fig.32). Along the ridge of the LATTENGEBIRGE to HINTER SCHONAU. From SCHONAU to the KÖNIGSEE by train (Fig.33), up the WASSERFALL weg, avoiding Lager DÜRRECK, which is inhabited by employees of the Stollenbaukp (chiefly Roumanians). Up the HOHES BRETT. This mountain is very dangerous in winter, but can be negotiated in summer without ropes. Up to the wire south of the KEHLSTEIN BERG.

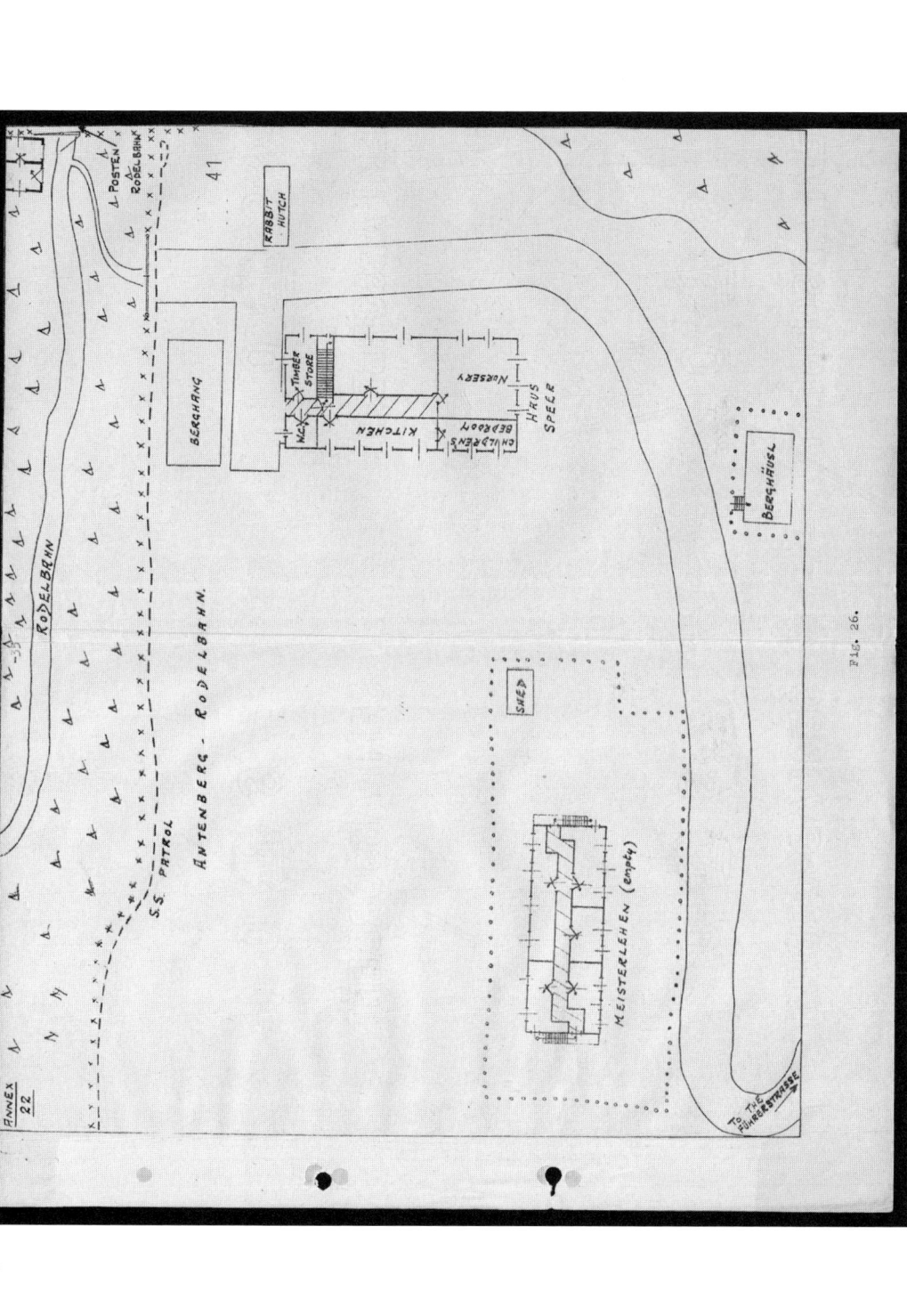

Fig. 26.

ANNEX 21.

ATELIER "SPEER"

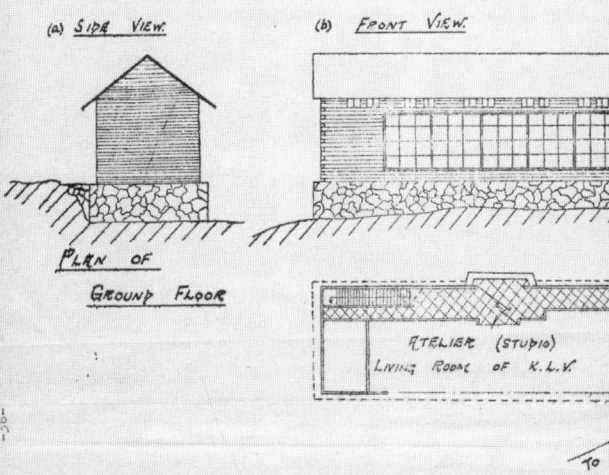

(a) SIDE VIEW.   (b) FRONT VIEW.

PLAN OF GROUND FLOOR

ATELIER (STUDIO) LIVING ROOM OF K.L.V.

BEDROOM OF K.L.V.

TO THE FÜHRERSTRASSE

FIRST FLOOR.
BEDROOMS AND LIVING ROOMS OF K.L.V. (Evacuated children).

SPEER'S STUDIO HAS BEEN TAKEN OVER BY THE K.L.V. AND NOW HOUSES EVACUATED CHILDREN FROM BOMBED CITIES.

ANNEX-IV

BAUMGARTLEHEN (Pigsty of the Gutshof)

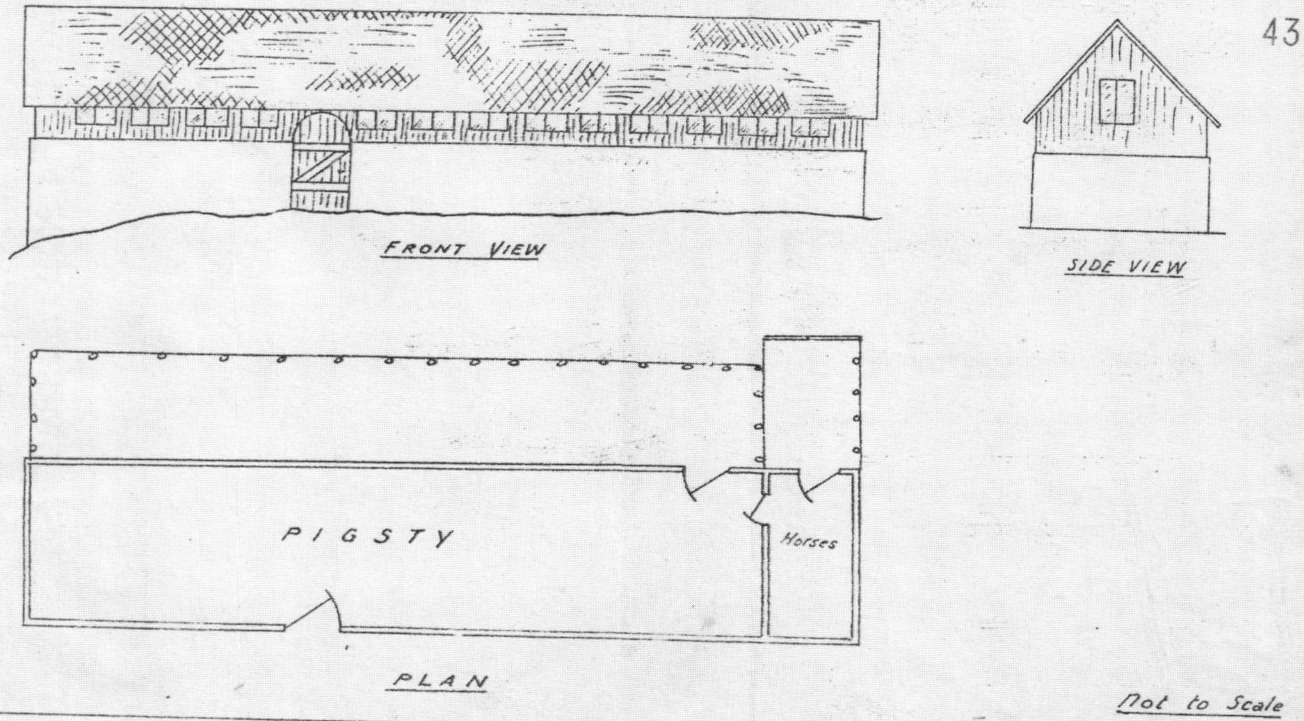

FRONT VIEW

SIDE VIEW

PIGSTY

Horses

PLAN

Not to Scale

Fig. 28.

ANNEX 6

- 38 -

"GUTSHOF" OBERSALZBERG

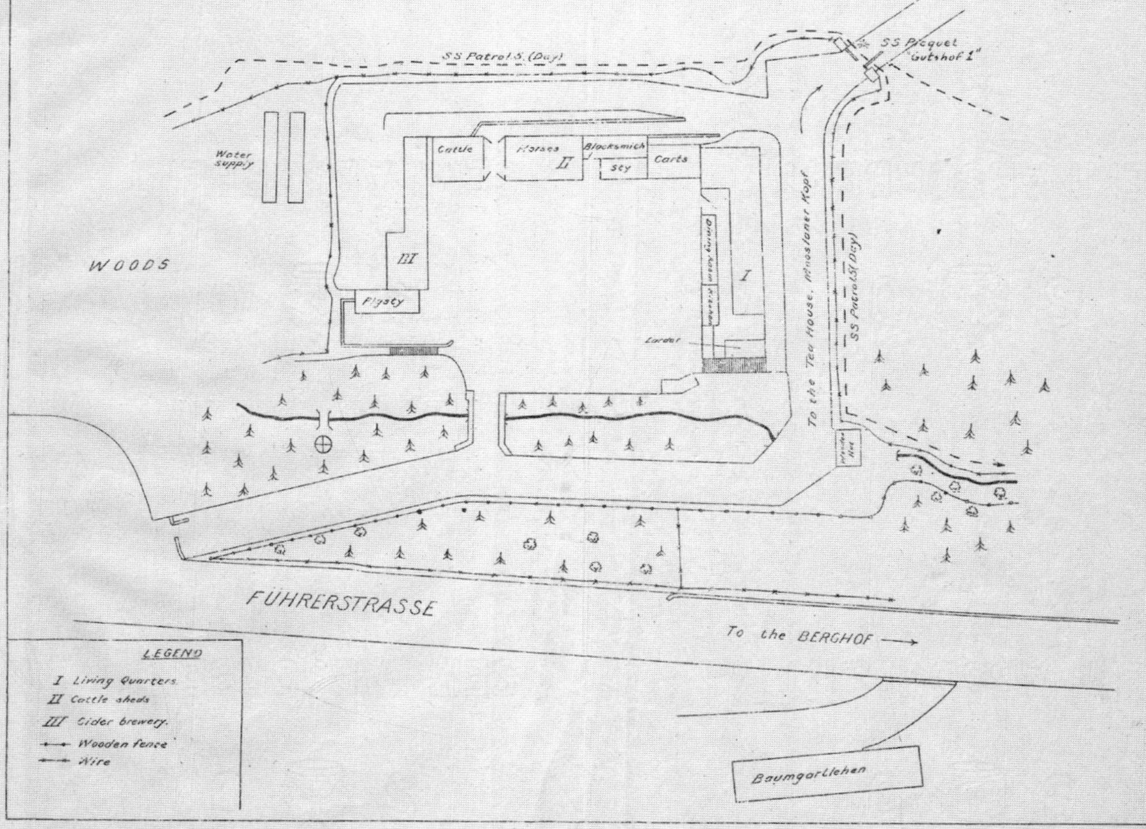

Fig. 29.

LEGEND
I Living Quarters
II Cattle sheds
III Cider brewery
•—•—• Wooden fence
—×—×— Wire

Key to Fig. 30.

1. Bergwerk.
4. Halt Berchtesgaden Ost.
11. Bahnhof (railway station).
19. Franziskaner Kirche.
23. Rathaus.
25. Pfarrkirche.
26. Stiftskirche.
33. Berchtesgadener Hof (Grand Hotel).
34. Protestanishe Kirche.
46. Villa Alpenglühen.

Fig. 31. BAD REICHENHALL and aerial railway up to the
PREDIGSTUHL.

Fig. 32. BAD REICHENHALL and the PREDIGSTUHL.

Fig. 33. Panorama showing Berchtesgaden, Berghof, ("Hitler's Landhaus"), Schönau, Königsee and WATZMANN.

At midday and in the evening the RSD men eat, when they retire into the house and the wire can be climbed. In the evening the game-keeper has also left. Alternatively one can go via the PURSCHELIA Haus on to the road leading down from the OFENER Alp or on to ROSSFELD (Fig.1). There are AA positions at both these places and there was formerly a camp for Czech workers on the OFENER ALP. This, however, no longer appears to be in existence, having collapsed under the weight of snow last winter. There are numerous small huts along the side of the road leading down from the OFENER ALP, each inhabited by two men who work the AA smoke screen, but one can get down through the woods, coming out by Lager RIEMENFELD (Fig.2).

(2) An alternative approach is to take the railway from SALZBURG to St. LEONHARD (Fig.1). Take the BERCHTESGADEN bus to UNTERAU and walk in by way of OBERAU (Fig.2).

From the Bergwerk near BERCHTESGADEN the Gutshof can be approached by way of the WASSERSCHLÖSSL, (Fig.1) but dog patrols have to be reckoned with. To get into the Führergebiet (within the wire) itself is more difficult. The SS guard mounts at 1300 hrs, so that all reliefs take place at every uneven hour. Patrol 5 therefore arrives at the Gutshof between 1000 and 1030 hrs. On one occasion a mad woman attempted to penetrate the area. By-passing Posten TEUGELBRUNN, she climbed over the fence and got into the Gutshof, where she was arrested.

An alternative approach is by the road leading round the north of GÖRING's house (Fig.2). Getting into GÖRING's house itself is easy, as the woods are so thick that the wire can be climbed unobserved. To cross the BERGHOF road without detection, is however, out of the question.

(3) There is a path from the Bergwerk near BERCHTESGADEN leading through two tunnels 1.80 m. high, which cannot be missed. It follows the south bank of the LAROSBACH (Fig.2), subsequently joining the Auerstrasse. It is possible to cut through the woods, travelling uphill, in the direction of the Teehaus on the MOOSLANER KOPF. The woods north-west of the FÜHRERGEBIET near the MOOSLANER KOPF are not, it is reported, patrolled either by RSD or SS personnel.

Alternatively, one can go over the LAROSBACH to the east of OBERSALZBERG (Fig.2).

Note: Fire brigade, civilian (strength about 120 men) in UNTERAU.

* * * * * * * * * *

Use of the buses from BERCHTESGADEN itself to the OBERSALZBERG is rather risky, as passes may be inspected, except on the workmen's buses on which the control is slack, the conductor merely shouting "Every-one got passes?" and apparently being satisfied with a chorus of "Jawohl's", he lets every-one get in.

The morning bus to the OBERSALZBERG leaves BERCHTESGADEN at about 1710-1720 hrs. and the midday bus at 1200-(1300?) hrs. There is also a workmen's bus (red) run by the Bauleitung Arge which leaves at 1500 hrs. The evening bus leaves at 1830 hrs, stopping at the Bergwerk in BERCHTESGADEN (Fig.30), UNTERAU, OBERAU (see Fig.1), KLAUSHÖHE and finally at the PLATTERHOF.

Buses leave the OBERSALZBERG at about 1000 hrs. and 1930 hrs. The red Bauleitung Arge workmen's bus leaves the Theaterhalle in the morning with workers for BERCHTESGADEN whom it brings back in the evening. (It returns at midday with the post, except in the case of important mail which arrives in the red mail truck (driven by an elderly man with a gold Party badge) and is driven direct to the Berghof).

6. Hideouts in the BERCHTESGADEN Area.

It is possible to stay at the TRIMBACHER and GOLDENER BÄR inns in Berchtesgaden, though the TRIMBACHER is frequented by the SS Wachkompanie, in particular the fire-fighting platoon. Other public houses in Berchtesgaden frequented (specially in the evenings) by the SS Wachkompanie OBERSALZBERG include the BRATWURSTGLÖCKL (innkeeper known as Michel) and the HOFSCHAFFER. Wachkompanie personnel when off duty also visit the Cafe ROTTENHÖFER, the Cafe GRASSL and the Cafe FORSTNER in Berchtesgaden. The BRATWURSTGLÖCKL is an ordinary public house where one can order a meal and put up for the night, though they do not normally take people in.

The TRIMBACHER, it may be noted, is the meeting place for most of the Czechs from Lager ANTENBERG and Lager RIEMENFELD. (Many of these Czechs work in Berchtesgaden as tradesmen; the barman at the GOLDENER BÄR is a Czech from Lager ANTENBERG.

It is possible to stay, without arousing suspicion, in the Haus BRANDTNER, which is the first house on the right from the Schiesstand bridge (Figs.1 and 30) on the Berchtesgaden-Obersalzberg road, before the Villa Alpenglühen is reached. There is, however, a Gendarmerie-posten at the Schiesstandbrücke.

There are further a number of sheds on the Hoch Lenzer (Fig.1) which can be approached either from Berchtesgaden or from the Königsee via DÜRRECK (avoiding the camp at Dürreck), and in which it is possible to hide. Similarly numerous empty sheds are to be found on the way from OBERAU to the OBERSALZBERG.

Hotels at present open in Berchtesgaden include the following:
         Das Deutsche Haus,
         Zur Post, and
         Berchtesgadener Hof.

The panorama in Fig.30 shows the location of several of the above.

In regard to the Obersalzberg itself, i.e. the immediate vicinity of the Berghof, there are, or were in May 1944, a number of abandoned habitations there. These include the Kamphäusl (Fig.23) and close to it, the Jugendverpflegungsheim (Fig.24) as well as the Meisterlehen (Fig.26), though access to all three is made difficult by the wire fence surrounding the Führergebiet, whilst the Jugendverpflegungsheim is uncomfortably close to the Führerstrasse. Both the Meisterlehen and the Jugendverpflegungsheim lie moreover in the open, unlike the Kamphäusl, which is partly surrounded by pine trees. If, as is reported, the Kamphäusl is never visited, the latter would appear to be the best hideout in the Obersalzberg itself - and a useful point from which to contact the Czech workmen in Lager Antenberg.

B. Protection of the Obersalzberg.

1. Security.

(a) Security Personnel. Security at the Obersalzberg is taken care of by the Reichssicherheitsdienst (RSD). There are about 20 men under the command of Brigadeführer RATTENHUBER. He is responsible for Hitler's safety and is always at his side. He is assisted by Hauptsturmführer MÜLLER, formerly of the Waffen SS.

RSD personnel usually wear civilian clothes. At other times they wear the uniform of the Waffen SS but with the shoulder straps of the Ordnungspolizei + unless they joined the RSD from the Waffen SS whose uniform they continue to wear. RSD personnel of the rank of Unterscharführer (the most common rank on the Obersalzberg) wear the Raute (a diamond-shaped patch of black cloth above the left cuff bearing the letters SD in silver embroidery.

+ intertwined silver, brown and/or green threads.

Fig. 34 shows an RSD officer of the rank of Hauptsturmführer in full dress. In winter RSD personnel (including officers) wear the SS Gebirgsjäger uniform shown in Fig. 35b, in common with Begleitkommando and Wachkompanie personnel.

RSD men at the Obersalzberg are mostly Bavarians.

The RSD patrol the entire Führergebiet (including the Kehlsteingebiet); they are usually accompanied by dogs of which there are three, each under the charge of a Hundeführer. One or two RSD men are said to be always at the Teehaus on the Kehlstein, which it is very difficult to reach except by the lifts.

There is also an RSD-Kommando at Berchtesgaden, where RSD men are always to be found hanging about the Railway Station which is carefully watched.

(b) Passes. Passes are dark blue, and all require a stamp (which is numbered) to be affixed every week. Passes bear the imprint of BORMANN's or RATTENHUBER's signature. Temporary passes may be signed by a minor official.

Personnel of SS Wachkp OBERSALZBERG have a special pass stating that they are members of the coy. and allowed into the Führergebiet on duty. They are recognised and consequently not checked. Children under 5 require no pass. The milkman, an employee of the Gutshof, and the woman who delivers the secret letters are never checked.

The following system of passes was in use in May 1944:-

(1) Führergebiet and Berghof. This pass is inscribed "ist berechtigt, das Führergelände und den Berghof zu betreten".

It is required in order to pass SS sentries 1 to 6 and any RSD personnel in the area.

(2) Führerstrasse. The part of the Führerstrasse which is closed to the public runs from Posten TEUGELBRUNN to Posten ANTENBERG. A special pass is required to pass SS sentry No.8 and the TEUGELBRUNN, BERGHOF and ANTENBERG civilian piquets. Passes of this kind are in the possession of the Czech and German workers employed in the area.

Passes are also possessed by the inhabitants of the Gutshof, Beckstein Haus, Berghang, Berghäusl, Atelier SPEER, and Haus SPEER.

The pass is marked: "ist berechtigt, die Posten TEUGELBRUNN und ANTENBERG zu passieren".

(3) Auerstrasse. A pass is required to leave the Führerstrasse and enter the SS barracks area past the civilian piquet at Posten AUERSTRASSE. This pass is marked: "ist berechtigt, Posten Auerstrasse zu passieren".

(4) Theaterhalle. A special pass is required to attend shows at the theatre hall. Such a pass is in the possession of every inhabitant of the OBERSALZBERG.

Fig. 34. RSD officer of the rank of Hauptsturmführer.

(5) **GÖRING's House and SS Barracks area.** Pass inscribed "ist berechtigt, den Posten KLINGECK zu passieren". In the possession of all who work in the SS barracks and the Vordereck.

Whilst GÖRING is in residence, Piquet GÖRING 1 is instructed to be particularly conscientious. All officers who visit GÖRING must produce evidence of having been invited. Those who wish to see GÖRING in a hurry can go to Posten KLINGECK, where they are taken to the RSD, and provided by the latter with a temporary pass.

(6) **KEHLSTEIN.** To enter this area a pass must be specially stamped "... und KEHLSTEINGEBIET".

2. Troops.

These include the following SS units:-
The SS Führerbegleitkommando; the SS Wachkompanie OBERSALZBERG (SS Kommando OBERSALZBERG); the SS Sonderkolonne (MT); and the SS Nebelabteilung (Smoke unit).

(a). **SS Führerbegleitkommando.**
Distinction must be made between the Führerbegleitkommando (Führer's escort detachment, who are SS personnel) and the Führerbegleitbataillon, which usually provides the guards at FHQ/OKW, and is a unit of the Division Grossdeutschland.*

The only Division Grossdeutschland personnel at OBERSALZBERG are the telephone operators at the Gästehaus Hoher Göll.

The Führerbegleitkommando consists mainly of SS officers and senior N.C.O.s with only a few other ranks. Some are always at the Chancellery at Berlin, others at the Berghof, and a few at FHQ, i.e. on the Führerzug (Hitler's train). The 20 at the Berghof live in the Vordereck and in the servants' quarters at the Berghof.

They are distinguishable from other SS personnel by the superior quality of their uniforms. NCOs wear uniforms of officer pattern. Führerbegleitkommando personnel wear an arm-band above the left cuff bearing the inscription "Adolf Hitler"; the golden arm-band with the word "Führerhauptquartier" is no longer worn.

Fig.35a shows the full dress uniform of a Gruppenführer such as TIEFENBACHER, who commands the SS Führerbegleitkommando, would wear. In winter and on less formal occasions all ranks wear Gebirgsjäger trousers (stuffed into ski boots) and the Bergmütze with the Totenkopf (death's head emblem) in front, as shown in Fig.35b. The letters LAH are worn on the shoulder straps.

The Führerbegleitkommando personnel at the Berghof are mostly Bavarian.

---

* Guard duties at Schloss KLESSHEIM were on occasion performed by a detachment of 2 NCOs and 20 men from the Wachkompanie, OBERSALZBERG. It is possible that Schloss KLESSHEIM is therefore only at times used as Führerhauptquartier.

Fig. 35a. Uniform of SS Gruppenführer TIEFENBACHER of the SS Führerbegleitkommando.

Fig. 35b. Uniform of an Unterscharführer of the SS Führerbegleitkommando.

The SS Führerbegleitkommando is commanded by Gruppenführer TIEFENBACHER, who is also responsible for guarding the Führer's train.

(b). **SS Wachkompanie OBERSALZBERG** (formerly SS Kommando OBERSALZBERG).

The SS Kommando OBERSALZBERG or Führerschutzkommando as it was once called, was formed in 1938 and subsequently became the SS Wachkompanie OBERSALZBERG. It is nominally under the direct control of Himmler. A considerable proportion of the guard company (70%) has been at OBERSALZBERG since the beginning of the war. A few men have been sent from time to time to other divisions, a practice which has become more frequent of late. There have also been exchanges of personnel, particularly with the SS Mountain Division. Nowadays no-one is promoted to NCO without previous service at the front. The personnel vary considerably, most of them being Austrian and Bavarian, though the nominal role also includes Germans from the Sudetenland and Upper Silesia as well as Volksdeutsche from Roumania.

The men are drawn from all the old SS formations whose particular arm-bands they continue to wear on the left sleeve. Letters denoting unit, e.g. SKD or LAH are no longer worn on the shoulder straps. The uniform worn by personnel of the Wachkompanie is shown in Figs. 36 and 37.

The company was commanded (April/May 1944) by Obersturmführer UBART, though for administrative purposes it comes under Sturmbannführer FRANK, commanding the SS Kommando, OBERSALZBERG. (The duties of the SS Kommando OBERSALZBERG are purely administrative; its strength is about 30 men, all of whom are clerks).

The strength of the Wachkompanie is about 180 men. (For armament, see under 6. Air Raid Precautions below).

One of the platoons is a fire fighting platoon (Feuerlöschzug) of 3 sections, viz. one on duty, one standing by on the Büchenhöhe and the other off duty or performing guard duties. It is the duty of the fire fighting platoon nightly to provide a patrol of 3 men to check the black-out. This duty is carried out at varying times but not after 0200 hrs.

Dress: field service, steel helmet, but no arms.

The Wachkompanie also furnishes the personnel for the Bergwacht, a patrol of 5 to 6 men which goes out when there is an accident in the mountains.

Reveille for the Wachkompanie is at 0700 hrs.
Field post No.; Wachkp. OBERSALZBERG 03951.

(c) **SS Sonderkolonne** (Dienstwagenhalle).
This is the SS unit which supplies drivers and mechanics etc. and MT for Hitler and his entourage. It consists of 3 Züge (platoons), viz. one at FHQ, another at PULLACH, near Munich, numbering about 40 men, and one Zug at the OBERSALZBERG, strength: 60-80 men. This platoon, in addition to providing drivers and M.T. for Hitler's entourage also does

Rottenführer
SCHÖNICKLE.

Rottenführer
MÜLLER.

Unterscharführer
WENERT.

Officer of the
guard an Unter-
sturmführer from
local AA defence.

Unterscharführer
GALLAU.

P/W informant.

Fig. 36. Guard of honour furnished by SS Wachkompanie Obersalzberg on the occasion of King Boris' last visit to the Berghof.

Fig.37. SS Schütze of Wachkompanie in overcoat.
(Outside Reichskanzlei, Berlin).

all the driving for the SS-Kommando OBERSALZBERG and the Wachkompanie as well as for the Air Raid-Shelter Construction Co., for whom they fetch gravel from HALTHURN on the BERCHTESGADENER- BAD REICHENHALL road. The commander of the SS Dienstwagenhalle at OBERSALZBERG is Obersturmführer KREIDERER. Under his care are the 6 Mercedes-Nürburg cars used by Hitler's entourage and two of the new Hitler cars.

(d) SS Nebelabteilung.
This unit, which consists of three troops (Battalion) each of 80-100 men, is commanded by Hauptsturmführer SCHWEIGER, but like the Wachkompanie, comes under the administrative control of the SS-Kommando OBERSALZBERG. The personnel are distributed about the countryside, two to a hut. Smoke equipment consists of small holders, a gas flask and a stove pipe. The apparatus is put into operation by turning a handle, except for apparatus in the Führergebiet, which is operated electrically.

3. Piquets and Patrols.(see Fig.2).

Two types of piquets and patrols exist at the OBERSALZBERG, viz. SS and civilian.

(a) SS piquets and patrols.
These are provided by the SS Wachkompanie OBERSALZBERG.

(1) SS piquets (see Fig.2).

No.	Place.	Weapons.	Remarks.
1.	Haus Türken	Automatic pistol(FN)	-
2.	In front of the Berghof.	"	Only at night. A number of RSD personnel in vicinity piquet very strictly.
3.	At entrance to the Berghof.	"	Alarm devices to Haus Türken When Hitler is at the Berghof there is also an Untersturmführer at this post. On arrival at this gate Hitler's chauffeur gives one toot on the horn, Bormann's chauffeur two and the gate is thrown open.
4.	Behind servants' quarters at Berghof.	"	--
5.	Gästehaus.	Rifle '98.	It is possible to get into the back of the Berghof through the Gästehaus.
6.	"Idiotenhügel" between Gästehaus and and Berghof.	"	Has good view of approach from Berghof to Gästehaus.
7.	?		Presumably no longer exists.
8.	At loading ramp to Führerstrasse.	"	
9.	Maierhaus.	Automatic pistol(FN)	-
10.	Theaterhalle.	Rifle '98.	Six men-reliefs for sentries in the theatre hall itself. During a show RSD personnel and entire Bereitschaft (squad ready to turn out for duty at any time) of the Wachkompanie as well.

SS piquets (contd.).+

No.	Place	Weapons	Remarks.
G1.	At gate to Gärtnerei (see Fig.38)	Pistol	When GÖRING is in residence the piquet exercises stricter control.
G2.	In front of GÖRING's house.	Machine pistol	Night and day because of air raid shelter.
G3.	Behind GÖRING's house.	MG34 on tripod	Only at night.
	Gutshof.	Rifle '98	Chief duty to watch over Hitler during his early morning walks (to Teehaus) Can see Hitler for part of walk at distance of 800-1000 m. Kept informed of morning walks.

It is possible that the system of piquets described above has been revised since April/May 1944 and that sentries are instead now placed at the entrances to the air raid shelters which were under construction at that time (see Fig.2, etc.).

(2) **SS patrols.** These are on one-man patrols. All patrols carry rifles and are relieved every 2 hrs. Some of the routes taken by the patrols are given below:-

> Patrol 1: BERGHOF to MOOSLANER KOPF. The patrol is relieved at the BERGHOF. The beat takes 15-20 minutes. Patrol chats for a long time with the civilian piquet at the MOOSLANER KOPF.
>
> Patrol 5: SS piquet post 3 to civilian piquet at TEUGELBRUNN. Patrol crosses bridge over stream until he is within sight of the civilian piquet at TEUGELBRUNN but he does not go right up to his post. By night he patrols up to the MOOSLANER KOPF. (Alarm telephone and bells on trees).
>
> Patrol Gästehaus to Piquet Post 3.
>
> Patrol Posten ANTENBERG to Posten RODELBAHN. Patrol along wire. He can see down to the Führerstrasse except where it is screened by trees.
>
> Patrol Bienenhaus: Operates only when Hitler is at the Berghof.
>
> Patrol Kehlstein: When Hitler is at the Berghof, area north of Kehlstein patrolled in winter by one pair of SS guards at a time.

+ Extra piquets are provided when Hitler is at the Berghof viz. one in front of and outside his study and another behind the Berghof.

(b) <u>Civilian piquets and patrols</u>.

(1) <u>Civilian piquets</u>. These are mostly Bavarian or Austrian. They look like ordinary workmen and are a very mixed type, but reliable Nazis of high standing. They stand on duty in sentry huts (see Fig.39) and wear civilian clothes without any distinguishing marks. Apparently they are not armed. Civilian piquets are stationed at the following points:-

- (i) Posten TEUGELBRUNN
- (ii) Posten AUERSTRASSE
- (iii) Posten RODELBAHN (wooden sentry box) Easy to get past piquet if approached in the right way.
- (iv) Posten ANTENBERG. Stands in open to check traffic entering and leaving ANTENBERG.
- (v) SS Barracks. Two civilian piquets are on duty at the KLINGECK.

(2) <u>Civilian patrols</u>. The only civilian patrols are the lumberjacks and a gamekeeper who wander round the KEHLSTEIN.

4. <u>Wire</u>. (see Fig.2).

Fences in and around the FÜHRERGEBIET are built of mesh wire and are 200/220 cm. (about 7ft.) high; they are supported by steel tubes placed at intervals of 3-5 m. The tubes are bent over inwards at the top, the bent part carrying 3-4 strands of barbed wire.

There are numerous gates in the wire - also of wire mesh - all of which are locked except those covered by guards. There is no electric current in the wire. As far as is known there are no trip wire or automatic alarm apparatus.

The KEHLSTEINGEBIET is also completely wired off.

5. <u>Anti-Aircraft Protection</u>. (see Figs.1, 2, 30).

Anti-aircraft guns are sited as follows:-

(a) At the end of the road leading to the OFENER ALP (part of a troop)
(b) Directly next to the ROSSFELD Hütte (remainder of above troop).
(c) At SCHÖNAU (one troop, men of which are billeted at the KOHLHIASL, an inn).
(d) Directly opposite the Bergwerk at BERCHTESGADEN, at the far side of the Ache in bend of the river (one troop).
(e) At the Dietrich Eckart Hütte near DÜRRECK (one troop).
(f) On the LOCKSTEIN, BERCHTESGADEN.

The guns are mostly 8.8 cm. calibre. There are no searchlights. There is also a section of 4-barrelled A.A. guns on the OBERSALZBERG.(see Fig.2). All A.A. troops are under the administration of the SS-Kommando OBERSALZBERG.

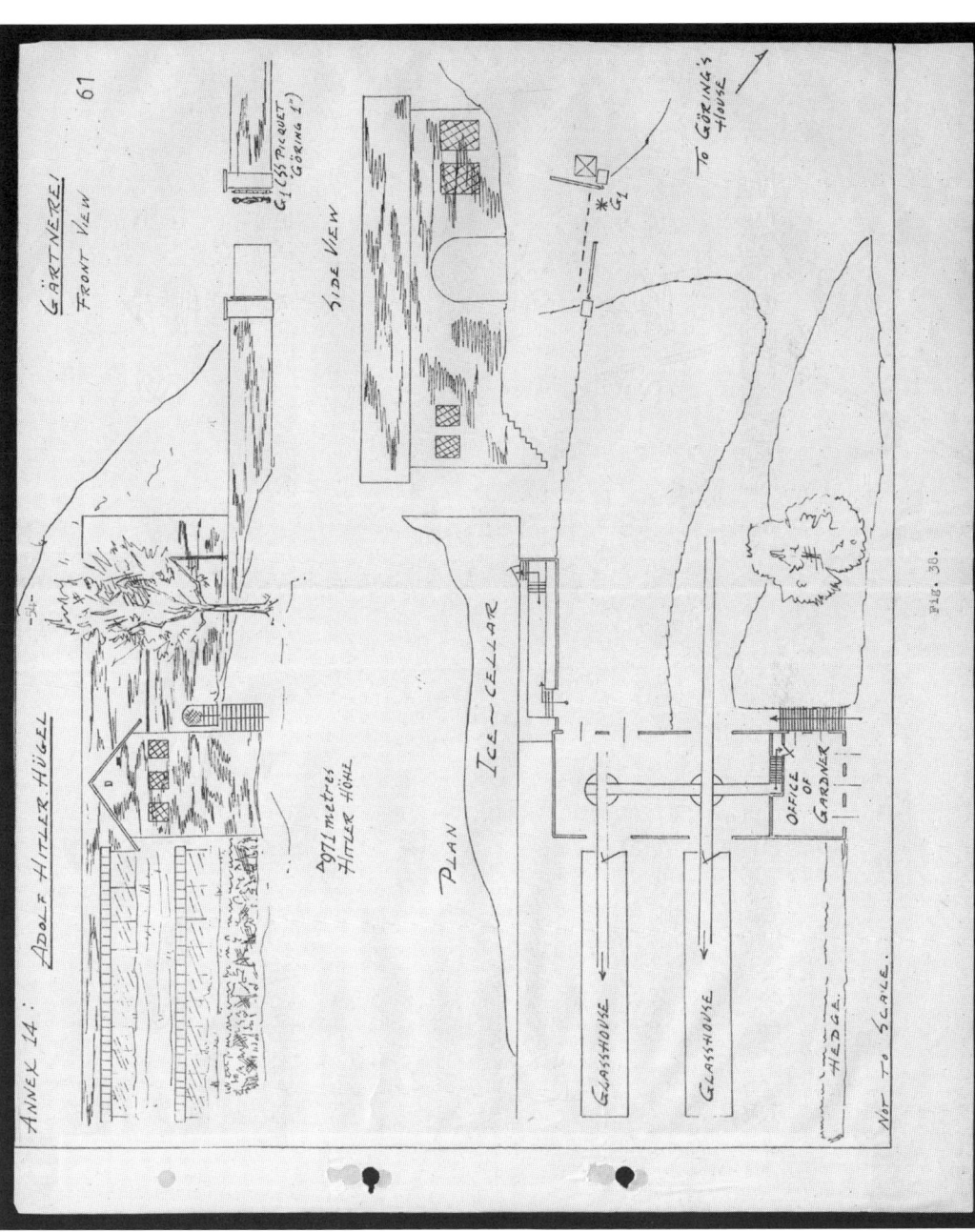

Fig. 30.

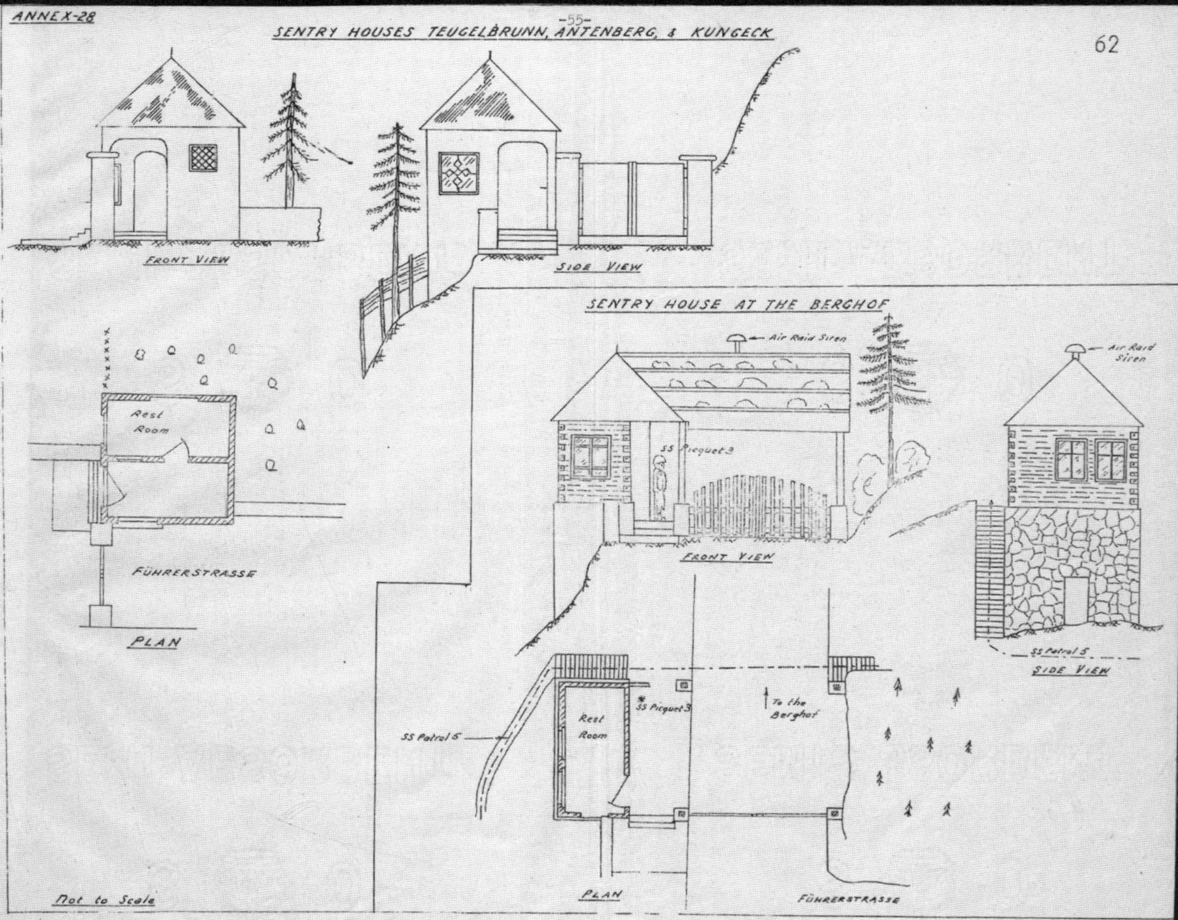
ANNEX-28
SENTRY HOUSES TEUGELBRUNN, ANTENBERG, & KUNGECK
FRONT VIEW
SIDE VIEW
Rest Room
FÜHRERSTRASSE
PLAN
Not to Scale
SENTRY HOUSE AT THE BERGHOF
Air Raid Siren
SS Picquet 3
FRONT VIEW
Air Raid Siren
SS Patrol 5
SIDE VIEW
SS Patrol 5
Rest Room
SS Picquet 3
To the Berghof
PLAN
FÜHRERSTRASSE

Fig. 39.

6. Air Raid Precautions.

(a) Warning System.

Warning of enemy aircraft is received direct from the Warnkommando, Travenstein and from the Party Chancellery at MUNICH. The warning system for OBERSALZBERG is under the control of Untersturmführer BREDOW with HQ in the second house of the VORDERECK.

Sirens are installed at the PLATTERHOF; at House 20 on the KLAUSHÖHE and probably at the BUCHENÖHE. They give the following signals:-

(1) **Vorwarnung** (Alert) also called the "Öffentliche Luftwarnung" (Public Alert): 3 deep long blasts lasting one minute in all. This means single aircraft over the area or aircraft in direct flight towards the area but some distance away.

(2) **Flieger Alarm**: Wailing sound signifying aircraft in area (given even when a few aircraft have become detached from formations attacking MUNICH, for example).

(3) **Vorentwarnung**: (First All Clear). As for (1) signifying that main body of raiders has passed.

(4) **Entwarnung**: (Second All Clear). High-pitched blast lasting one minute.

When the public alert is sounded a special warning in the form of 3 short rings repeated twice is given on the following telephones:-

Ext. 383 U.v.D. (Unteroffizier vom Dienst) or orderly NCO.
Ext. 369 Fencing Room i.e. fire piquet
Ext. 333 Equipment (fire-fighting) room.

The above extensions are at the SS Barracks.

Also Ext. 202 (Untersturmführer BREDOW).
Ext. 283 Klaushöhe. Fire-fighting squad.

(b) Air Raid Shelters. (see Fig.2).

Vast air raid shelters were built into the mountain side at OBERSALZBERG in 1943/44. HITLER's and BORMANN's shelters were completed in May 1944. All shelters are to be linked up.

HITLER's shelter runs under the Berghof and is 15-20 m. underground: it zig-zags at the entrance, turning left, left again, then right, where it reaches the main passage. The shelter itself is 80-100 m. long with rooms leading off at either side. It has a parquet floor and carpets, and is sumptuously furnished and centrally heated by a boiler built-in underneath the shelter. The shelter is ventillated but there are no air shafts. It has 3 exits.

In addition to air raid shelters there are several observation shelters on the OBERSALZBERG (see Fig.23). Protection consists of 15-20 cm. of reinforced concrete. It was reported in April 1944 that they were all to be connected by telephone.

(c) Camouflage. Apart from being treated to resist fire, all buildings at the OBERSALZBERG are reported to be sprayed with paint in a disruptive pattern which is changed every 3 months.

C. Personalities in the OBERSALZBERG and their habits.

1. Hitler.

(a) Appearance. Photographs of Hitler, who is now 55, often show such changes in appearance that one is tempted to credit the popular belief that he has one or more doubles. Thus the air of good health, calm and collected bearing mentioned by officers visiting FHQ in 1943 contrasts with the description of officers actually serving there at the time, that the Führer was looking 10 years older. The photograph in Fig.40 showing the Führer in his train was taken in 1943 and bears out the report at first hand of Hitler looking grey and bent in May 1944; yet the photographs in Figs.41a and 41b of Hitler after the attentat of July 20th, 1944, indicate the very reverse. How much these changes in appearance are to be ascribed to the frequent injections given the Führer, who is in general well-known to enjoy poor health, or to the employment of a double, it is impossible to say, evidence on the latter point being particularly conflicting.

Hitler's dress varies from the greenish-khaki jacket and breeches seen in Fig.36 for instance, such as he usually wears out-of-doors on formal occasions, to the brown or grey double-breasted jacket and black trousers that he normally affects indoors and at the Berghof.

Apart from the Iron Cross Hitler wears no military decorations.

Fig.40.

Der Führer bei den Verletzten des 20. Juli

Lazarettbesuch nach dem ruchlosen Anschlag bei den verletzten Mitarbeitern und Angehörigen des Wehrmachtführungsstabes

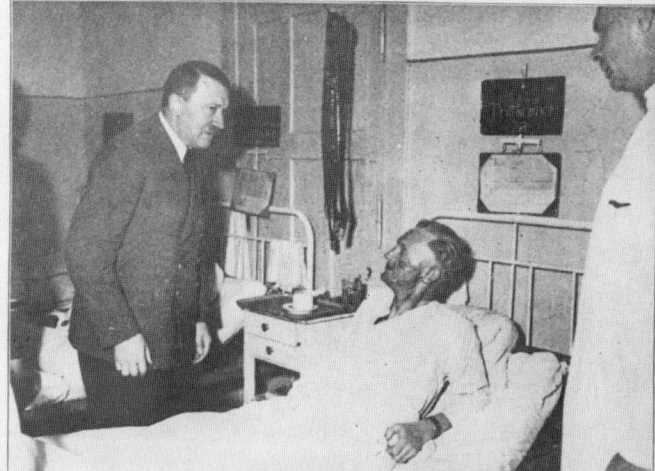

Konteradmiral v. Puttkamer, langjähriger Adjutant der Kriegsmarine beim Führer.

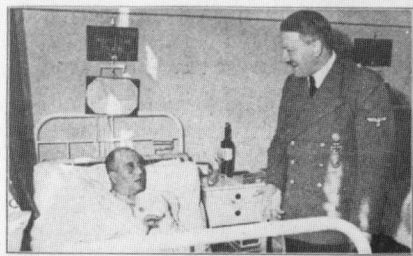

General der Infanterie Buhle

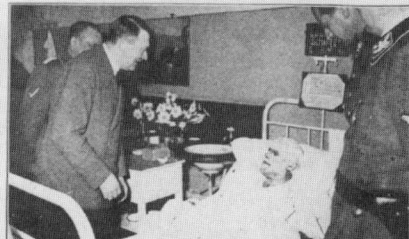

Generalmajor Scherff

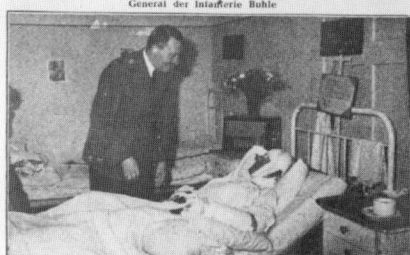

Kapitän zur See Aßmann

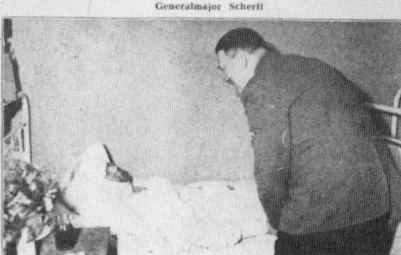

Eichenlaubträger Oberstleutnant Borgmann

Fig. 41a.

Reichsleiter General Ritter von Epp machte sich zum Sprecher der Parteiführerschaft, indem er mit bewegten Worten der Freude Ausdruck gab, den Führer nach dem ruchlosen Anschlag von 20. Juli in voller Gesundheit und Schaffenskraft zu sehen.

Von links: Reichsleiter General Ritter von Epp, Reichsführer ⚡ Himmler, der Reichsbevollmächtigte für den totalen Kriegseinsatz, Reichsminister Dr. Goebbels, Reichsleiter für die Presse Amann, Reichsminister Dr. Frick, Reichsarbeitsführer Hierl, Reichsminister Rosenberg, Reichsleiter Bouhler und Reichsleiter von Schirach.

Der Befehlshaber des Heimatheeres, Reichsführer ⚡ Reichsinnenminister Himmler, im Gespräch mit dem Reichskommissar für Norwegen, Gauleiter Terboven.

Der Chef des Wehrmachtführungsstabes, Generaloberst Jodl, unterhält sich mit Reichsminister Backe und Gauleiter Hofer.

Der Führer spricht mit dem Generalbevollmächtigten für den Arbeitseinsatz, Gauleiter Sauckel.
Aufnahme: Presse-Hoffmann

Der Führer verabschiedet sich nach der Kundgebung der Treue und des gläubigen Vertrauens, die ihm die Parteiführerschaft bezeugte.

Fig.41b.

(b) **Hitler's doubles.** Evidence is conflicting of the truth of this popular rumour. The only confirmation comes second-hand from a Gestapo official, who describes in some detail his surprise at seeing the Führer pass him twice (in the same direction) within a few minutes at the Reichkanzlei in Berlin and first-hand from a number of the Wachkompanie of the SS Leibstandarte Adolf Hitler. In the latter instance, the double is described as a Ministerialgehilfe employed at the Reichskanzlei, Berlin, who wore the prescribed uniform of brown jacket and black trousers and was so much the exact double of Hitler as frequently to be mistaken for him and saluted by the SS guards. It is possible that it is this person who was referred to by the Führer as the "collaborator BERGER" killed in the bomb attempt on Hitler's life of July 20th 1944 at MUNSINGEN (another of the FHQs). On the other hand the evidence of another SS Leibstandarte man who was one of Hitler's three body servants from 1936-1940 refutes the above report of one or more doubles.

(c) **Routine at the Berghof.** Hitler is a late riser, never getting up before 0900 or 1000 hrs. He is first seen by his barber, after which he either goes for his morning walk to the MOOSLANER KOPF, or attends a conference. He always walks alone +
to the MOOSLANER KOPF, strolling in a fairly leisurely manner. The walk takes 15 to 20 mins. at normal pace. There is an SS guard at each end and an SS patrol (one man) patrolling the route. Hitler cannot bear to feel himself watched, and if he sees an SS man following him about, he shouts at him "If you are frightened, go and guard yourself". In consequence guards have been instructed to keep him in sight but to remain unobserved themselves. This order has, however, been countermanded and reinforced several times. When Hitler is on this early morning walk an RSD official patrols the area with a dog. The route taken by Hitler on this walk to the MOOSLANER KOPF is shown in Fig.2.

When Hitler arrives at the Teehaus on the MOOSLANER KOPF, the SS guard or RSD official who is there on such occasions phones for the Kolonne,x (cars, adjutants, RSD, etc.), who meet him there. The tea-room is opened for him and he takes breakfast. Hitler <u>never</u> walks back, but drives with his Kolonne past the piquet Gutshof 1 along the Führerstrasse past piquet 3 into the Berghof.

+ In contrast with earlier days (1940) when it appears to have been Hitler's practice to take his walk at 1500 hrs. accompanied by BORMANN and SCHAUB (his personal adjutants) as well as by his aides-de-camp, the average number of the party rarely being less than twelve. The party was followed at a discreet distance by 6-10 guards. Two SD men were on duty at the Teehaus itself, where Hitler remained till 1830 or 1900 hrs.

x This Kolonne consisted in 1940 (when the same practice was that described above obtained) of 4-6 cars; Hitler always travelled in the leading car.

Otherwise Hitler breakfasts between 1100 and 1130 hrs. Breakfast normally consists of milk and toast. (Keka).

In the afternoon Hitler receives visitors: bearers of the Knights Cross, artists and other personalities, the arrival of whom must be previously notified. Dr. MORELL sometimes sees him in the morning.

If he has official visits he leaves by road for SCHLOSS KLESSHEIM at 1200 hrs. The cars are mostly Mercedes-Nürburg 6-seaters (see Appendix.). Hitler himself has two or more cars, which are armour-plated, with wind screen and side-screens 2 ins. thick. Colour: dark blue. Flies Führer's pennant on the right mudguard.

1600 hrs. - lunch. Vegetables only. Hitler would sometimes invite GÖRING or BORMANN's family to lunch.

After lunch Hitler works until 2200 hrs. usually with Eva BRAUN, who is fetched by telephone from the Gästehaus, or with a clerk.

2200 hrs. - conference on the military situation. The generals etc. used to arrive by car, via BAD REICHENHALL and BERCHTESGADEN, entering the Berghof at piquet post 3, where they were all checked. They were stopped first by the gendarme at the SCHIESSSTANDBRÜCKE, who noted who they were, as they had no pass, and telephoned Posten TEUGELBRUNN, who in turn telephoned piquet 3. Generals were sometimes asked for a lift by personnel of the Wachkp. who found themselves at the SCHIESSSTAND-BRÜCKE.

0100 - 0130 Hitler has supper. As for lunch.
0300 - 0400 or later he goes to bed.

When arriving at or departing from OBERSALZ-BERG, Hitler always travels by his special train, which has a quadruple 2 cm. AA gun at each end. He usually drives down to SCHLOSS KLESSHEIM, and leaves from there; sometimes, however, from BERCHTESGADEN via BAD REICHENHALL. The train is usually stationed at SCHLOSS KLESSHEIM. There are three other special trains, - RIBBENTROP's, KEITEL's (which is stationed at BISCHOFSWIESEN, where there is supposed to be a magnificent chancellery), and the guest train which fetches guests from SALZBURG or from the aerodrome at AINRING to BERCHTESGADEN.

Hitler used to go up the KEHLSTEIN at one time but seems to have dropped this practice of late.

+ See attached Appendix. I...Hitler's Cars.

x Up to 1940, lunch was served at 1400 hrs.; dinner being served between 1930 and 2130 hrs.

2. Other personalities in the OBERSALZBERG.

(a) Martin BORMANN. (Fig.42). Born 1900. Chief of Staff of the Chancellery of the Party (Stabsleiter der Partei-Kanzlei) and member of the War Cabinet, BORMANN simultaneously holds the rank of SS Gruppenführer and SA Gruppenführer. By calling a farmer, he became, after World War I, a member of the notorious Rossbach Freikorps and was connected with several FEME murders. Until 1941 he was HESS's right hand man and succeeded HESS in office after the latter's flight to Scotland. BORMANN is in supreme control of the OBERSALZBERG in Hitler's absence. He is not popular and is known locally as the "Black Shadow on the Mountain" (Schwarzer Schatten am Berg). He rarely leaves the OBERSALZBERG and nearly always wears civilian clothes, viz. grey trousers tucked into boots, grey jacket and soft hat.

Frequently seen in 3-axle touring car (usually with a horde of children in the back), which he drives himself. He does not drive nor permit others to drive at over 30 m.p.h. in the OBERSALZBERG.

Fig.42.
(Bormann in centre).

(b) Heinrich HIMMLER. A rare visitor to the Berghof which he visited for instance in the period August 1943 - May 1944 only twice, being accompanied on one occasion by SS Oberstgruppenführer Sepp.DIETRICH. Moved about everywhere without a guard and was not challenged in any way by the patrols. On both occasions he left the same day as he arrived.

(c) Hermann GÖRING. GÖRING is the successor designate to Hitler, Chairman of the War Cabinet, member of the Privy Council, Reich Minister for Air etc.

He is a fairly frequent visitor to the OBERSALZBERG where he stays, at times for considerable periods, at the Landhaus Göring. He is always accompanied by a Luftwaffe Feldwebel (Sergeant), and his chauffeur is an Oberleutnant of the Luftwaffe. General der Flieger BODENSCHATZ is his frequent companion though GÖRING walks about a good deal alone. Does not appear to be carefully guarded.

(d) Joachim von RIBBENTROP. Reich Minister for Foreign Affairs; member of the Privy Council. Rarely goes nearer to the Berghof than SCHLOSS KLESSHEIM. He has a villa at FUSCHL.

(e) Albert SPEER. Reich Minister for Armaments and War Production and Chief of the Organisation Todt, etc. Is rarely at the OBERSALZBERG although his family reside there in the Haus Speer.

(f) Dr. Otto DIETRICH holds the rank of SS Gruppenführer and is Reich Press Chief of the Nazi Party. He is a frequent visitor to the OBERSALZBERG where he stays at the Gästehaus HOHER GÖLL. As Staats-Sekretär in the Reich Ministry of Propaganda, he is GOEBBELS's representative at BERCHTESGADEN. Frequently seen in uniform as well as in mufti.

(g) Julius SCHAUB (Fig.43) holds the rank of SS Obergruppenführer and is one of Hitler's personal adjutants. His place at the OBERSALZBERG appears to be taken by Brigadeführer ALBRECHT as he is rarely seen there nowadays.

Fig. 43.

(h) Alwin ALBRECHT is like SCHAUB a persönlicher Adjutant des Führers and holds the rank of NSKK Brigadeführer. He generally wears uniform.

(i) RATTENHUBER holds the rank of Brigadeführer and the post of Chief of the Reichsicherheitsdienst at the OBERSALZBERG. Age about 50; lives in the Gästehaus HOHER GÖLL. He is responsible for Hitler's safety and rarely leaves his side.

(j) <u>Eva BRAUN</u>, Hitler's secretary. Age about 24; brunette, attractive and unconventional in her costume, sometimes wearing Bavarian leather shorts. Walks around with two black dogs, generally in the company of Frl. SILBERHORN, telephone operator at the Gästehaus, when off duty. Several RSD personnel always in the background when she goes out. Unapproachable, no make-up (Hitler, it appears cannot tolerate the use of cosmetics). Until 1942, (if not later) lived in the Berghof. Relations with Hitler now appear to be of a platonic nature.

(k) <u>General der Flieger Karl BODENSCHATZ</u>, is the Chief of GÖRING's personal staff and resides in the Adjutantür Göring at the OBERSALZBERG. He usually wears civilian clothes and drives his own Mercedes, in which he willingly gives anyone a lift.

(l) <u>Dr. Karl BRANDT</u> is Plenipotentiary General for Health and Medical Services, holding simultaneous ranks of SS Brigadeführer and General-major der Ordnungspolizei. He is Hitler's doctor in BERLIN and is a rare visitor to the OBERSALZBERG or FHQ, where Dr. MORELL acts as Hitler's physician. BRANDT is 170 cm. in height and slim. Frequently wears the uniform of a Major-general of the Ordnungs- polizei.

(m) <u>Dr. MORELL</u>, Hitler's personal physician at the OBERSALZBERG. Age about 60; corpulent, medium height, with grey hair standing up like a brush.

(n) <u>Gruppenführer TIEFENBACHER</u> is in command of the Begleitkommando.

(o) <u>DÜHRING</u>, Major-domo, at the Berghof, where his wife acts as housekeeper.

(p) <u>Hauptsturmführer MÜLLER</u> of the RSD. Age about 30; height 1.87 m.; dark, short hair, noticeably dark complexion. Formerly in the Waffen SS, whose uniform he wears with a WIKING armband on left cuff.

(q) <u>Obersturmführer UBART</u> in command of the SS Wachkompanie in May 1944.

(r) <u>Sturmbannführer FRANK</u> chief of the SS Kommando OBERSALZBERG. Generally seen in mufti.

(s) <u>Sturmbannführer SPAHN</u> head of the SS Verwachung OBERSALZBERG and is assisted by -

(t) <u>Untersturmführer BREDOW</u> chief of Air Raid Control.

(u) <u>Hauptsturmführer SCHWIEGE</u> commands the smoke unit (Nebelabteilung) at the OBERSALZBERG.

(v) <u>Obersturmführer KREIDERER</u> in charge of the SS Dienstwagenhalle.

(w) <u>Obersturmführer VATER</u> of the SA is responsible for looking after guests visiting the Berghof, assisted by 3 LAH men - WEISS, SCHNEIDER and BUSCHMANN.

(x) <u>Frau SCHAPLYTZEL</u> is Hitler's personal cook at the Berghof.

D. Possibilities of action in the Berchtesgaden area.

In the absence of first-hand information on the OBERSALZBERG since May of this year and in particular since the attentat of July 20th, it is not possible to say whether security and safety measures have been tightened up of late, or whether extra precautions are being taken at FHQ only.

The possibilities of action in the Berchtesgaden area considered below are based on the conditions obtaining there in May 1944.

1. Timing.

The readiest indication of Hitler's presence in the OBERSALZBERG is the big swastika flag which is flown on such occasions from the flagpole at the car park in front of the BERGHOF.+ Amongst other view-points this flag is visible from the SCHELLENBERG-UNTERAU road (Fig.1), the Cafe ROTTENHÖFER (Fig.30), and the DOKTORBERG, both in Berchtesgaden.

Another indication is the presence in the neighbourhood of the various Sonderzüge (special trains), viz. Hitler's at Schloss KLESSHEIM sidings (Fig.61), Keitel's at BISCHOFSWIESEN, the Gästezug (visitors' train) at Berchtesgaden and Ribbentrop's train at Salzburg (Fig.62).

A third clue to Hitler's presence at the OBERSALZBERG is provided by the clientele of the Wirthaus HOFSCHÄFNER (Fig.30) in Berchtesgaden, a tavern much frequented in the evening by members of the SS Führerbegleitkommando when off duty.

2. Suggested course of action.

It is evident from the notes given under C.1.(c) of Hitler's routine that two opportunities present themselves of liquidating the Führer, firstly when on his way to and from the Teehaus on the MOOSLANER KOPF and secondly when en route to or from Schloss KLESSHEIM.

In neither case would the operation be an easy one or without peril, particularly in the former instance, i.e. the MOOSLANER KOPF, for here not only have we to reckon with wire fences but with SS piquets and patrols as well as the RSD dog patrol.

(a) **Action at the MOOSLANER KOPF** (Fig.2). Action here is nevertheless worthy of consideration in view of the fact that whereas a considerable interval of time may elapse between Hitler's visits to Schloss KLESSHEIM and other FHQs ˣ the Führer rarely misses

---

+ P/W informant, ex-SS Wachkompanie Obersalzberg, is emphatic on the existence of this flag and on the fact that it is <u>only</u> flown when Hitler is at the Berghof.

x In 1943 and the earlier part of 1944 (i.e. before the invasion of France and during the lull on the Russian front) Hitler is said to have remained at the Berghof for weeks on end. This is unlikely to be the case nowadays, when his departures from the OBERSALZBERG may well be as frequent as his walks to the MOOSLANER KOPF.

his daily walk to the teahouse on the MOOSLANER KOPF (30 in Fig.2). Thus from the middle of March 1944, before which date the snow was too thick, Hitler went to the Teehaus nearly every day.

Hitler is reported to set out from the Berghof for the Teehaus between 1000 and 1100 hrs. following the route marked in Fig.2. Walking alone, the Führer is under observation throughout his walk by the SS patrol which follows him at a discreet distance. Hitler is also under the observation of the SS piquet at the GUTSHOF for about 1000 yards of the walk, and is visible to the SS piquets at the Theaterhalle and the Landhaus Göring as he crosses the concrete by-pass from the OBERAU road to the Führerstrasse. These piquets are, however, well over 500 yards away.

The modus operandi suggested is as follows:-

(i) Approach: From the LAROSBACH (Fig.2) through the woods to the wire fence near the point at which the concrete by-pass cuts the route followed by Hitler in his walk. The operative or operatives (supposing two snipers are employed) should be in position, (say) between this point and the teahouse, not earlier than 1000 hrs. (to give RSD dog patrol time to have passed). The position taken up should be within 100-200 yards of the route.

(ii) Weapon and equipment: Mauser sniper's rifle, telescopic sight (carried in pocket), explosive bullets in magazine, wire-cutters (for making hole in wire fence), H.E. grenades carried in haversac for close protection and assistance in making get-away.

(iii) Disguise: Gebirgsjäger uniform. The great majority of the patients at the Lazarett (military hospital) in the PLATTERHOF are mountain troops. (Gebirgsjäger). Since the SS Führerbegleit-kommando, the RSD (when not in mufti) and the SS Wach-kompanie Obersalzberg all wear this type of uniform (Fig.35a) in winter (with slight modifications), impersonation on these lines would obviously facilitate approach to within striking distance. The modifications converting a Gebirgsjäger uniform into that worn by the SS personnel at the Obersalzberg are very quickly made. They merely consist of moving the Hoheitsabzeichen from above the right breast-pocket to the left sleeve above the elbow; removing the red, white and black rosette and Hoheitsabzeichen from the front of the Bergmütze and substituting for it the Totenkopf (death's head) emblem; changing the Wehrmacht collar patches for the SS flash and badge of rank (worn respectively on the right and left sides of the collar) - as shown in Fig.44, and perhaps removing the Edelweiss from the left side of the cap (Bergmütze).

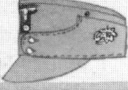 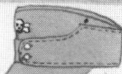

Bergmütze   Collar patch   Bergmütze   Collar patch Collar patch
                                          (right side). (left side).

Fig.44a. Gebirgsjäger.   Fig.44b. Unterscharführer of
                                  Begleitkommando or SS Wachkompanie.

(iv) <u>Alternative action at the Teehaus</u>. Assuming that the sniper failed and Hitler reached the teahouse unharmed, it might be possible to retrieve the situation, and even to regard the sniper's attempt as a diversion, by attacking Hitler in his car on the return journey to the BERGHOF. This attack would be made by two operatives firing a PIAT gun (or Bazooka) from the woods in the vicinity of the Teehaus. These operatives would not take up position until the arrival of the Kolonne at the Teehaus after observing the sniper's failure to bring down Hitler. They would thus avoid the risk of detection by any piquets and patrols in the neighbourhood of the MOOSLANER KOPF, whose attention would rather be drawn in the opposite direction. The Kolonne, one may reasonably assume, would be sent for post haste following the sniper's attempt. Whether Hitler returned alone to the Berghof or took his breakfast at the teahouse before returning, the guards would hardly expect a second attack to be made.

(b) <u>Action on the BERGHOF-Schloss KLESSHEIM road (Figs.1 and 2)</u>.

(i) <u>Place</u>: The route taken by Hitler when driving to Schloss KLESSHEIM is as follows:-

Out at Post No.1, past the AUERSTRASSE Posten, through OBERAU, UNTERAU, SCHELLENBERG, GRÖDIG, and thence on the Autobahn, circling SALZBURG, and skirting MAXGLAN.

As Fig.1 indicates almost the entire route from the Berghof as far as GRÖDIG is wooded. Except for a stretch of some 500 yards before reaching OBERAU and of about 100 yards on the other side of the village the Führerstrasse is heavily wooded all the way except for a few clearings. For a stretch of a kilometre in the vicinity of UNTERSTEIN the woods are described as particularly thick and come right down to the road.

The stretch of road north of SCHELLENBERG where the Führerstrasse rejoins the Berchtesgaden-Salzburg main road, appears from air-photos to have woods on both sides in close proximity to the road, i.e. between heights 925 and 1189, though the woods in the vicinity of St. LEONHARD-FELLARUNN have been cleared.

Adequate cover would therefore be available to a party armed with PIAT guns (or Bazookas) and H.E. and smoke grenades. (for close protection). The point chosen for delivering the attack should not only afford the necessary cover but preferably be situated at a sharp bend in the road which the Kolonne would be forced therefore to take at reduced speed.

(ii) <u>Guarding of route</u>. Until 1940 (at any rate) the road from the Berghof to Salzburg -(in those days via the Schiesssstandbrücke) was not guarded. More recent information (May 1944) indicate however, that the route from the Berghof via OBERAU, UNTERAU, GRÖDIG to Schloss KLESSHEIM (or Salzburg) is guarded by SS and RSD personnel. No details are available as to the spacing of sentries along the route or whether they are only placed at dangerous points. Intervals between guards (who must in any case be few in number) must be considerable.

(iii) <u>The Kolonne</u>. Before the war and certainly until well into 1940 Hitler's Kolonne usually totalled some 10 cars (see Appendix I), of which Hitler's was always the leading car. The latter was followed by 4 cars each carrying six SS guards with members of Hitler's entourage following in the remaining 5 cars. Since then the Kolonne appears to have been somewhat reduced in size, though it never consists of less than three MERCEDES-NÜRBURG 6-seater cars. The Kolonne is nowadays preceded (contrary to previous practice) by a RSD man on a motor-cycle or MC combination, who rides about 200 yards ahead of the leading car, and is armed with a Machine pistol. When motoring to Schloss KLESSHEIM Hitler usually rides in the second car and always in front+ alongside his chauffeur Obersturmführer KEMKA (Fig.   ), with Eva BRAUN and/or Brigadeführer RATTENHUBER of the RSD in the back of the car. He drives very fast in order to minimise the chance of being hit. The readiest means of recognising the car is by the pennant on the right-hand front mudguard (see Appendix I).

If instead of taking the Führerzug at the KLESSHEIM sidings Hitler takes the train at Berchtesgaden, the route followed will be the Führerstrasse to the SCHIESSSTANDBRUCKE (Figs.1 and 30) over the R. ACHE and thence to the station at Berchtesgaden (Fig.30), a route which likewise passes through well-wooded country affording good cover. In this case, however, the road is a good deal shorter than that to Schloss KLESSHEIM and therefore easier to guard.

(iv) <u>Timing of the attack</u>. The question of timing is considerably more difficult than in the case of the MOOSLANER KOPF. It would be necessary to keep the car-park in front of the Berghof under constant observation from 1000 hrs. onwards. This car-park is visible from the SCHELLENBERG-UNTERAU road. The numerous empty huts in the UNTERAU district might furnish usefull hideouts.

According to recent press reports Hitler has taken up his quarters in the Führerzug, which for safety is run into a tunnel. Attached as he is to the OBERSALZBERG Hitler is likely to continue to snatch as much time as he can there. The nearest tunnel to the Berghof is the one on the Berchtesgaden - Bad Reichenhall line (Fig.1) - apart from the tunnel reported to have been built under the Bavaria (Fig.30).

+ Hitler only rides in the back on ceremonial occasions, e.g. visits of foreign notabilities, Mussolini, for example.

In the event of Hitler spending his time between these tunnels and the BERGHOF (where deep air raid shelters exist), the Führerstrasse between Obersalzberg and Berchtesgaden would be the scene of the attack. Hideouts for the PIAT party might in this case be found in the empty huts on the Hoch Lenzer (Fig.1).

(v) <u>Disguise</u>. This would be the same as that mentioned above under D 2a (iii). In this case the operatives might pass themselves off as members of the Nebelabteiling (smoke unit) who are distributed in pairs over the whole Obersalzberg area.

3. Combined operation.

Assuming that it would be possible to learn some hours ahead of Hitler's presence at the OBERSALZBERG, a combined operation in the form of an aerial bombardment of the Berghof and the SS barracks accompanied by the dropping of a paratroop battalion (S.A.S.) whould be well worth while since it offers the best chance of eliminating the Führer as well as other leading Nazis in the OBERSALZBERG, Martin BORMANN, for instance.

Apart from the Wachkompanie, the Begleitkommando and the RSD with a total of about 260-280 all ranks, there would be little opposition, since the smoke and A.A. personnel are scattered over a very wide area. Most of the Begleitkommando and the RSD would moreover take to the air raid shelters in all probability, so that the Wachkompanie need alone be reckoned with. Opposition would, in fact, only be offered by the men standin-by for duty (Bereitschaft), the fire-fighting platoon, the piquets over the air raid shelters and patrols, and the residue of the Wachkompanie specifically told off for anti-paratroop duties. Apart from rifles, machine pistols, the armament of the Wachkompanie consists only of 12 Mg., 2 old 8 cm. mortars and a few 5 cm. mortars. A paratroop battalion could therefore swamp any resistance the troops guarding the OBERSALZBERG might put up.

Nor would it be possible for the garrisons of Salzburg and BAD REICHENHALL, assuming they still exist and have not already been sent to man the Western defences, to send help in time. Aerial bombardment could, in any case, be extended to Salzburg and Bad Reichenhall following the attack on the BERGHOF.

It was hoped at one time that this operation might be planned to take place in conjunction with a revolt by the foreign workers of the Salzburg area, in particular by French deportees and Ps/W, and Poles and Ostarbeiter, whose first action would have been to seize the arms depots in the Salzburg area marked 1,2,3, and 4 in Fig.1. There appears, however, little possibility of cooperation at the present time with the foreign governments in this connection.

Such information as is available on foreign workers in the Salzburg and Berchtesgaden areas is included in Appendix III.

Part II. THE FÜHRERZUG AS THE SCENE OF ACTION.

A. The Führerzug.

1. General Description.

Originally presented to the Führer by a group of industrial magnates, the train has been used by Hitler, not only on official visits to the heads of other Fascist governments, e.g. Mussolini and Franco, but also as a mobile headquarters when visiting the various theatres of war.

The Führerzug may be distinguished from the other special trains (Sonderzüge) used by Ribbentrop, Keitel, and Himmler, for example, by its colour, which is described nowadays as a dirty violet or very dark blue (approaching black). Until recently its colour was darkish green like that of the other Sonderzüge.[+] It is streamlined and appears to be lower than the normal German train. The chief features which distinguish the Sonderzüge (and the Führerzug) from ordinary Reichsbahn or Mitropa rolling stock are their larger windows, wider concertina gangways between coaches, their superior coachwork, the 1½ ins. white stripe under the windows and at the bottom of the panelling along the whole length of the train (see Figs.47 and 48), and the telephone connections between coaches.[x]

It has been said, and the statement has been confirmed, that the Führerzug is sometimes divided into three parts, viz. an advance train (Vorzug) with the code name KLEINASIEN, a main train (in which Hitler nearly always travels) with the code name AMERIKA, and a rear train (Nachzug) with ASIEN as its code name. No information is available regarding distance and/or time between parts, though on one occasion the main train (Hauptzug) is said to have left SALZBURG 1½ hrs. (0930 hrs.) after the Vorzug (0800 hrs.). Informant has stated that the main train can be distinguished from the other two (at close quarters) by the telephone wires from the two locomotives which link up with the train as far back as the W/T coach, and by the disruptive pattern painted on the roofs of the coaches as camouflage. Another distinguishing feature is that only the part in which Hitler travels is believed to have a saloon coach. It is not unlikely that the three trains are only used on special occasions. They are, for example, said to have been repainted (dark green) at POTSDAM during the spring of 1942, prior to Hitler's journey to HENDAYE to meet Franco. The first train is described as carrying various members of Hitler's staff, with Hitler and his immediate entourage, including the Begleitkommando in the second train and security police in the third.

[+] Though a reliable source describes Göring's special as a dirty violet in colour.

[x] These are described as only visible between coaches and even then as difficult to see.

Another informant who was one of Hitler's body-servants (Bursch) until mid-1940 and frequently travelled on the train denies the existence of duplicate Führerzüge. Nor were the latter met with on the Eastern Front (Polish Corridor) during the Russian campaign (see Appendix IV below). The nearest approach to anything of the kind is the advance train, which, according to three Austrian railwaymen well acquainted with Sonderzug procedure, always precedes, in Germany at any rate, every Sonderzug. This advance train consists of a locomotive with one or two coaches carrying railway police (Bahnpolizei) who are set down to reinforce the local railway police when necessary.

2. Composition of the Führerzug.

Disregarding any question of advance, main and rear parts, the Führerzug as used by Hitler to travel between Freilassing, Salzburg (Berchtesgaden, Schloss Klessheim railhead) and the various FHQs consists of two locomotives and some 14 coaches.+ The composition of the train in 1940 is given as follows:-

No. of coach from front to rear.	Description.
1.	Forward Flak (A.A.) coach.
2,3.	Begleitkommando.
4.	Dienstpersonal (train staff).
5.	Telephone and W/T coach.
6.	Secretariat.
7.	Bormann and his staff.
8.	Dining car and kitchen (Mitropa).
9.	Adjutants.
10.	Hitler's saloon coach.
11,12,13.	Various high personages.
14.	Rear Flak (A.A.) coach.

Another (later) report describes the Führerzug as consisting, in 1943 (during the Russian campaign), of two locomotives and 10-11 coaches. In this case the sequence from first to rear is given as follows:-

Coach with armoured cupola mounting tank gun or MG
Flak (A.A.) coach mounting quadruple (Vierling) AA gun
6-7 coaches of the Pullman type
Flak (A.A.) coach with quadruple A.A. gun, and another coach with armoured cupola mounting tank gun or MG.

In 1941 the Führerzug at Schloss Klessheim sidings was described as consisting of about 20 coaches. In neither of the examples given are luggage vans included (unless certain of the coaches incorporated luggage compartments) and it is possible that the Führerzug, like Ribbentrop's special train, has luggage vans at either end of the train.

+ Figures given vary from 6 to 9-10 and even 20 coaches.

The coach marked Dienstpersonal is probably a Salonpackwagen as on Ribbentrop's train. Comparing the two trains the chief difference is the inclusion of two dining cars on Ribbentrop's train, though part of one, it is true, is used as the Secretariat. The Secretariat coach on Hitler's train may therefore be of the same type (see Fig.56). The position of the W/T coach on Hitler's train is not known for certain and it has been placed in front of the Secretariat coach as the most likely place. In Ribbentrop's train of 14 coaches it is the eighth car from the front. Not only coaches 11. 12. and 13. but Bormann's coach may on occasion drop out, so that the figure of 9-10 coaches given for Hitler's train may therefore be correct at times.

Fig.45 shows the Führerzug entering the Anhalter Bahnhof, Berlin, on Hitler's return from France in 1940, and gives some idea of the length of the train with its two locomotives.

Fig.45. The Führerzug entering the Anhalter Bahnhof on the occasion of Hitler's return to Berlin after the Battle of France.

This photograph gives some idea of the length of the train with its two locomotives.

Fig.46 shows a view of part of the train at SUBOTICA, 1941, on the occasion of Hitler's 52nd birthday, whilst Figs.47 and 48 give a close up view of the coaches and the white stripe below the windows and at the base of the panelling. This is also visible in Fig.49, which shows Hitler leaning out of the window of his saloon coach. Fig.50 shows one of the locomotives which, as Figs.51 and 52 indicate, is followed immediately by the S.A. coach.

Fig. 46. The Führerzug at SUBOTICA (20th April 1941) on the occasion of Hitler's 52nd birthday.

-74-

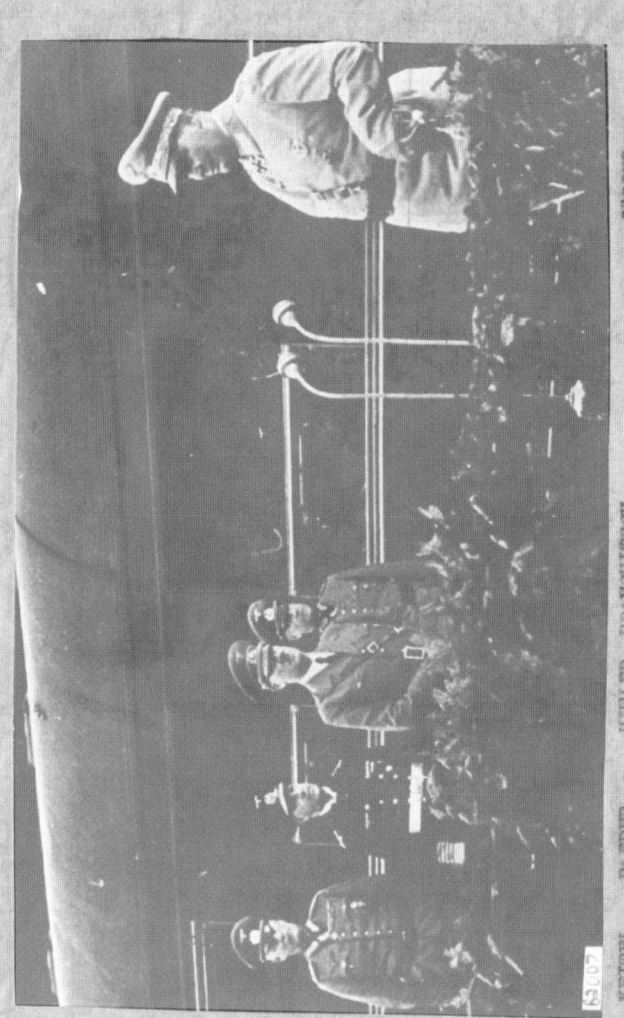

KEITEL   RAEDER   HITLER   BRAUCHITSCH   GÖRING.

Fig.47. Führer's coach at SUBOTICA (20th April 1941).

Brigadeführer ALBRECHT.

Fig.48. Another view of the Führer's coach (Subotica - 20th April 1941).

Fig.49. Hitler leaning out of the window of his Salonwagen.

Note: The distinguishing white stripe below window along whole length of coach and at bottom of panelling, characteristic of all special trains including the Führerzug. Painted darkest green like all Sonderzüge, the colour of the Führer's train is now reported to have been altered to dark blue or violet.

Fig. 50. Locomotive of Führerzug (Anhalter Bahnhof, Berlin, July 1940).

Fig. 51. Locomotives and Flakwagen (A.A. coach) of the Führerzug (Anhalter Bahnhof, Berlin, July 1940).

Fig.52. Flakwagen (A.A. coach) of the Führerzug
(Anhalter Bahnhof, Berlin, July 1940).

3. The coaches of the Führerzug.

The internal layout of certain of the coaches on the Führerzug is described below, and shown in Figs. 53-58.

(s) <u>The A.A. coaches.</u> The layout of each of the
A.A. coaches (on Ribbentrop's train) is shown in
Fig. 53 below. It is believed to be identical with
that of the Flakwagen on Hitler's train.

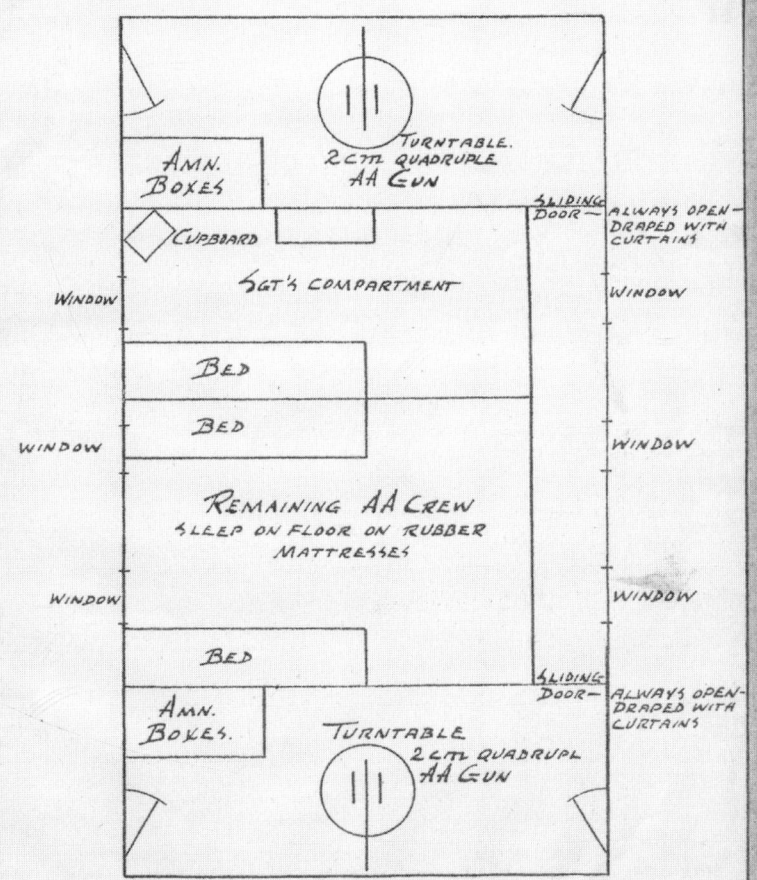

Fig. 53.

(b) <u>Salonpackwagen</u>. (Dienstpersonalwagen). The layout of this coach is shown in Fig.54 below.

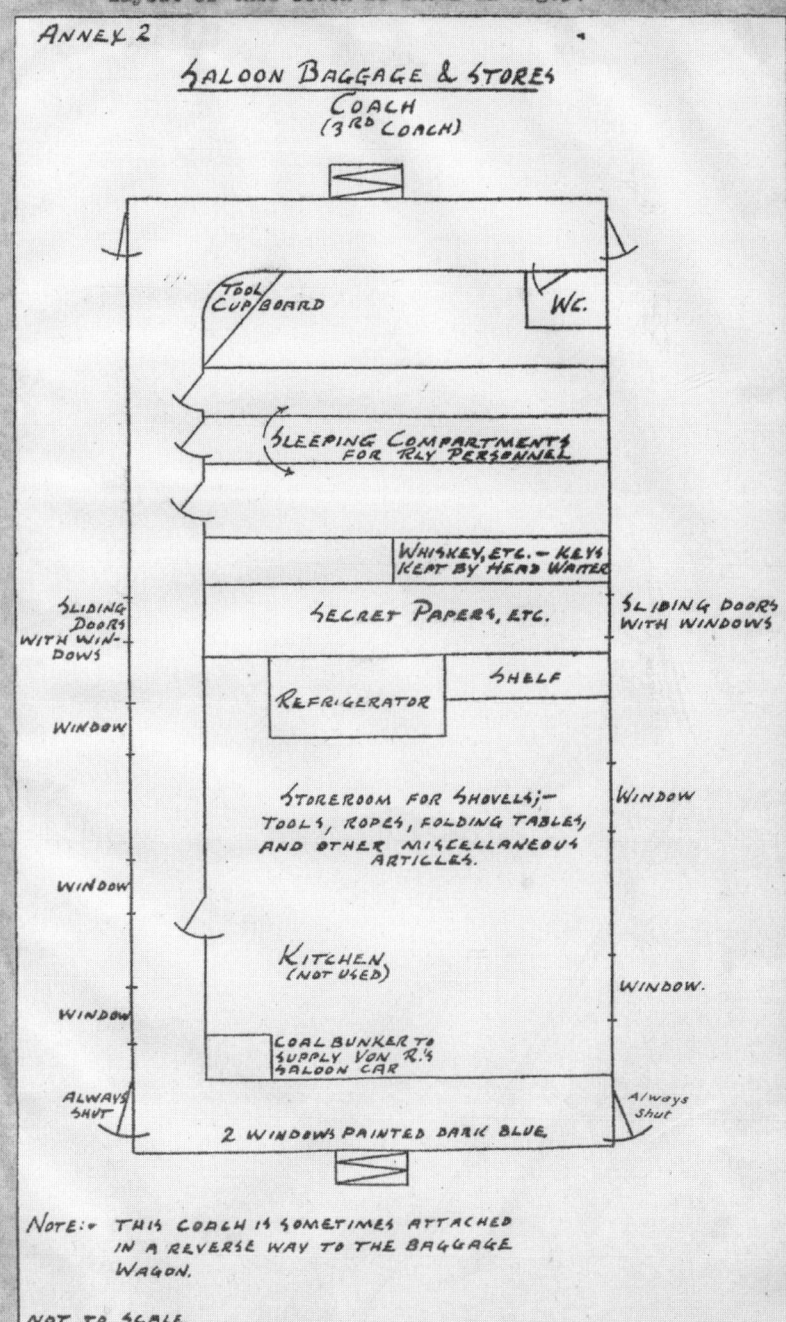

Fig. 54.

(c) <u>The W/T coach</u>. The interior of the W/T coach
on Ribbentrop's train is shown in Fig.55. On the
assumption that this is standard for all Sonderzüge,
the one on Hitler's train will have the same layout.

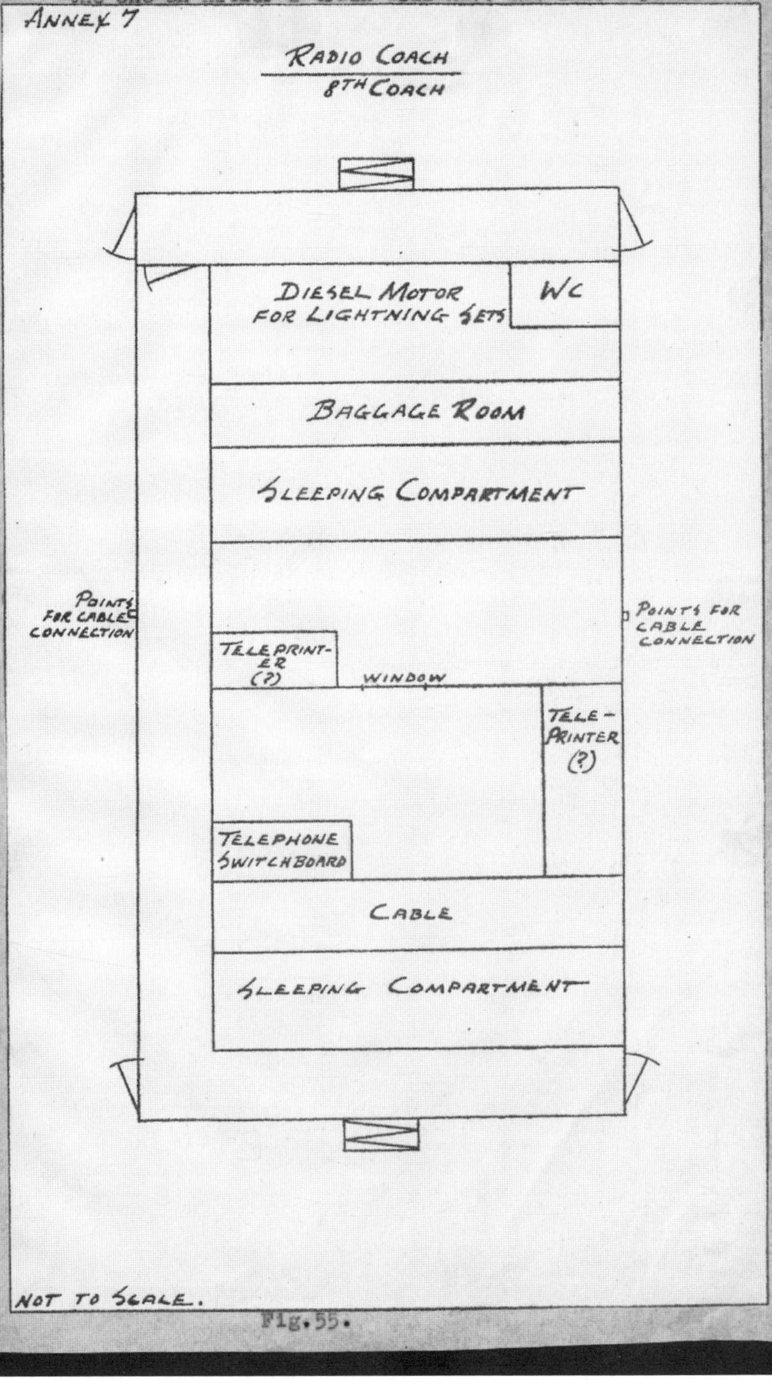

ANNEX 7

Radio Coach
8TH COACH

DIESEL MOTOR FOR LIGHTNING SETS	WC

BAGGAGE ROOM

SLEEPING COMPARTMENT

POINTS FOR CABLE CONNECTION — TELEPRINTER (?) | WINDOW — POINTS FOR CABLE CONNECTION

TELE-PRINTER (?)

TELEPHONE SWITCHBOARD

CABLE

SLEEPING COMPARTMENT

NOT TO SCALE.

Fig. 55.

(d) <u>Secretariatwagen</u>. On Ribbentrop's special train this coach is a converted Mitropa dining car, and it is not unlikely that much the same arrangement has been adopted on Hitler's train for accommodating the Führer's secretaries. The layout of this coach is shown in Fig.56 below.

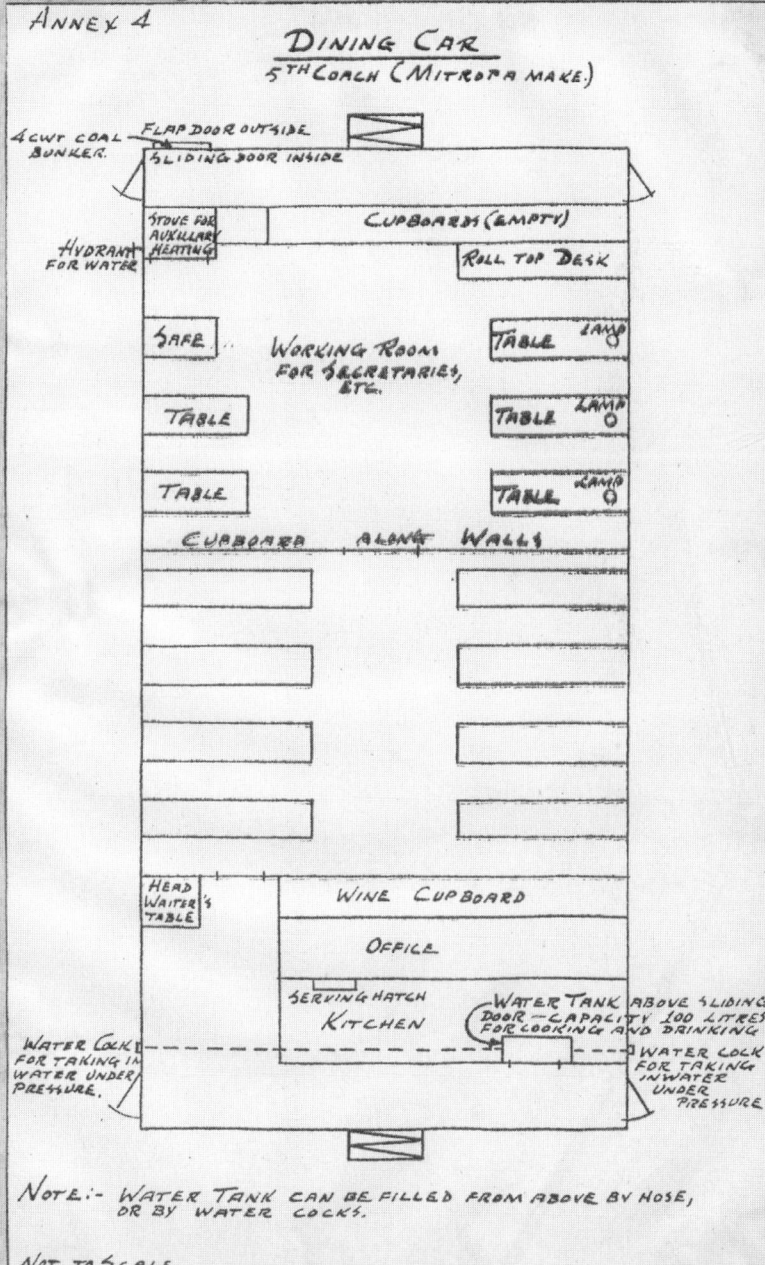

Fig.56.

(e) <u>The dining car</u>. Assuming this to be of same type as in Ribbentrop's train, the layo[ut] be that depicted in Fig.57.

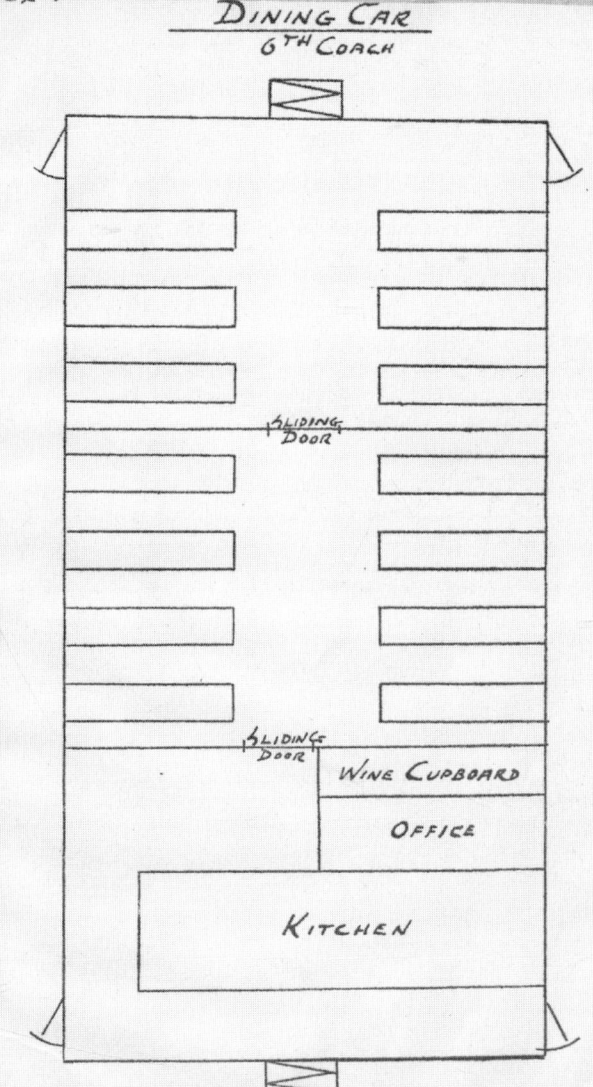

Fig. 57.

(f) <u>Hitler's Salonwagen</u>. The internal arrangement of this coach (in 1940) was that shown below in Fig.58. The bed itself is said to be of the tip-up type.

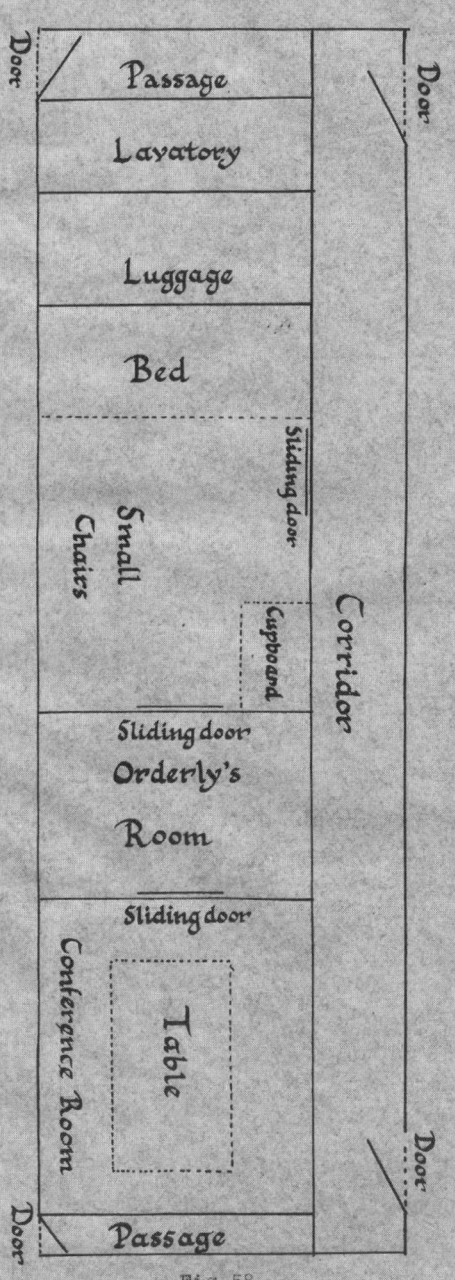

Fig.58.

B. Protection of the Führerzug.

1. Protection on the train itself.

(a) **En route.** The Begleitkommando on the train is about 20 strong, of whom two-thirds are SS Leibstandarte personnel and the remainder Sipo/SD (Gestapo)+ men. Two men are always on duty at the entrances at either end of Hitler's coach. At stops the Begleitkommando descends and forms a bodyguard round Hitler, never leaving his side. (see Fig.59).

The total strength of the train personnel, including Flak and Begleitkommando, waiters, and railway employees is 100-120.

Fig.59. Hitler leaving the Anhalter Bahnhof on his return to Berlin from France (July 1940) followed by the Begleitkommando.

(b) **In the sidings.** (FREILASSING, Schloss KLESSHEIM, or SALZBURG). The only details available on the guarding of Sonderzüge are those applying to RIBBENTROP's special train. In this case four of the Flak personnel are on guard during daylight; at night the train is guarded (at SALZBURG) by two Bahnpolizei armed with pistols, who patrol the line on either side of the train. When Hitler is at FHQ the Führerzug appears to be guarded by a detachment from the Führerbegleitbataillon of the Grossdeutschland Division.

2. Guarding of the route.

This includes stations and track (tunnels, bridges, signal boxes, points, etc.).

+ Frequently wearing mufti.

(a) <u>Stations</u>. According to four out of five
informants, platforms are not usually cleared of
civilians either by day or by night, when a Sonderzug stops or passes through the station, nor are
special guards mounted on stations through which
Sonderzüge run non-stop (in this case the train is
stated usually to go through on a line not adjacent
to the platform). According to one informant a
certain number of railway police, train and local
Gestapo (some in mufti) are, however, always on
guard when the train stops. These men walk up and
down the platform at which the train is standing,
Bahnpolizei being also stationed on the remoter
platforms. The only restriction laid on civilians,
according to another informant, is that the police
try to clear the public back on the platforms (as
shown in Fig.60), but when the train stops, the
crowd throngs right up to the coach to try to touch
the Führer (as shown in Fig.49). This information,
it is true, dates from 1940, when Hitler was in his
heyday, and it is possible that safety measures
have been tightened up of late, and that the Bahnpolizei now allow no-one near the train; they are
also said to see that railway employees servicing
the train do not loiter unnecessarily.

Stops at stations are said to last as long as
half an hour.

Fig.60.

(b) <u>Track</u>. In Russia, as in other occupied territories,
it has been the practice to guard the line heavily
with Bahnpolizei (and if required troops), with
sentries every 100-200 m. during the passing of a
Sonderzug. This has not, at any rate until recently,
been the practice in Germany, though the rails may
be inspected by a Reichsbahn official.

The guarding of the railways in Austria appears to be slacker than elsewhere in the Reich. Signal boxes are not guarded as a rule, bridges and tunnels are guarded by the military, and stations by the Bahnpolizei.[+] Guards at bridges and tunnels are said to consist of only two men and to be very slack in performing their duties.

The guarding of railways in occupied territory in the early stages of the war (1941), according to the account of an attempt by a Polish resistance group to blow up Hitler's train in West Prussia (Polish Corridor) given in Appendix IV, was also carried out by Bahnpolizei. The latter are stated to have patrolled the line from time to time, but to have spent most of the time near the points and signal boxes, (the latter being quite close to the points they operate). The Bahnpolizei normally carried out single patrols and were armed with rifles and hand grenades. Signal boxes were always too strongly guarded for any attempt to be made on them.

The bridges and stations were usually patrolled, but broadly speaking, there was little supervision in open country; patrols along the line were always made before Hitler's train was expected. In spite of these precautions this particular resistance group all but succeeded in their object.

(c) **Warning system**. A special time-table is made out for Sonderzüge and circulated by the Bahndirektion to the stations concerned via the Zugleitungen. This information is passed telegraphically. Information regarding the route and timing of Sonderzüge is stated to be in the possession of the Zugleitungen (Train Control) 12-24 hours ahead and of the minor stations about 30 mins. in advance.[x] The arrival of special trains is apparently announced by number only.

In regard to Hitler's train, the Zugleitungen and stations concerned are warned of the arrival of the train perhaps 3-4 hours ahead, others concerned only knowing about 20 mins. in advance. Sometimes the arrival of the Sonderzug is disguised by the announcement that it is a goods train, for instance, which is passing through. The arrival of Sonderzüge is stated by one informant to have been known to the local inhabitants of SALZBURG well in advance, possibly as a result of careless talk on the part of

---

[+] Railway police are normally armed with revolvers (sometimes with rifles or machine pistols). Uniforms are grey-green, army pattern, with a cog wheel on the black collar patch. Shoulder straps are of green and white intertwined cords, and also bear a cog wheel.

[x] At AMSTETTEN (AUSTRIA) for example, the railway officials were informed verbally some hours in advance that the special train was expected, though the full details did not arrive until 20 mins. before the train was due (Russians, French and Polish are employed on the railway at AMSTETTEN).

officials on the local Gauleiter's staff or perhaps the train staff.+

Lines are cleared for Sonderzüge only to the extent that the special train is not held up; in the case of Hitler's train all traffic, it has been said, is brought to a standstill and no shunting is allowed while the train is passing.

The railway staff responsible for supervising the passage of special trains is the Betriebswerkvorstand and the Amtsvorstand.

C. Servicing of Special Trains.

Servicing is here taken as including washing and provisioning.

1. Washing.

Coaches of von RIBBENTROP's train are washed outside SALZBURG station by half a dozen French women, the final wash being carried out the day before the train is due to leave. The interior is cleaned by Reichsbahn employees. The siding at which this operation is performed is shown in Fig.62. The Führerzug is usually serviced at Schloss KLESSHEIM by Führerbegleitbataillon personnel, though it has recently been seen on von Ribbentrop's siding at Salzburg, alongside GÖRING's train.

2. Provisioning.

(a) Water for drinking and cooking purposes is taken on at station stops en route between rail hydrants, the hose from the hydrant being either connected up from the fresh-water tank on the roof of the dining car (see Fig.64) or from water cocks on either side of the coach. The former procedure is adopted when there is not sufficient pressure behind the water supply.

When in the sidings at Salzburg, von Ribbentrop's train is shunted about 12 noon daily for this purpose from the main siding to a goods siding. Each coach is brought in turn past the hydrant between the rails, after which the train is taken back to the siding. The routine intake of water occupies about one hour. Similar hydrants are available at FREILASSING junction for the Führerzug when Salzburg is not used for the purpose of taking in water.

+ The following places of refreshment in Salzburg are frequented by train personnel (sleeping car attendants, waiters, engine drivers): Cafe BURGUND, the PITTER Cafe (on the first floor of the PITTER Hotel), the PITTERBRÄUSTUBL, and the Cafe MOZART in the Getreidegasse. This latter is also patronised by Führerbegleitbataillon personnel from Schloss KLESSHEIM, who also frequent the WALCHER MÜHLE in the MAXGLAN suburb of Salzburg. Places frequented by the SS Wachkompanie Obersalzberg in Salzburg include the MIRABELLE KASINO, the PLATZLKELLER, the ZUR TRAUBE, the GLOCKENSPIEL and the Cafe LOHR. The PITTERKELLER is frequented by Bahnpolizei. The French women responsible for washing v. Ribbentrop's train at Salzburg station are often to be found in the evening (after 5 p.m.) at the MOZART or PITTER Cafes or at the Cafe FÜNFHAUS, although they have be back at their Lager (camp) by 10 or 11 p.m. (They can be "dated").

(b) **Other supplies.** Beer, mineral waters, chocolate, malt and coffee used to be taken aboard at the Anhalter Bahnhof, sufficient quantities being delivered to last for 4-6 weeks. Potatoes and other vegetables as well as meat and fruit are usually delivered to the train at Salzburg.

All food and drink on the Führerzug are kept in the kitchen (cupboards). KANNENBERG, the Intendant at the Reichskanzlei is responsible for ordering food for the train in BERLIN and MUNICH. In BERLIN it used to be delivered by MITROPA though Hitler's food was specially brought from the Reichskanzlei in BERLIN or from the Berghof.

D. **Routeing of the Führerzug.**

Two routes are considered below, viz. to the north and to the west.

1. **To the north (BERLIN).**

The route followed by the Führerzug in travelling from BERCHTESGADEN or Schloss KLESSHEIM is as follows:-

BERCHTESGADEN
BAD REICHENHALL   or   Schloss KLESSHEIM

FREILASSING Junction

MÜHLDORF

LANDSHUT   or   MUNICH

PLAUEN

or

LEIPZIG   HALLE

BERLIN
(Anhalter Bahnhof).

Stops are made at LANDSHUT, REGENSBURG, HOF, LEIPZIG or HALLE (more often the latter). Special trains may also stop at JÜTERBOG or LÜCKENWALDE where Hitler, Himmler, Ribbentrop etc. with their entourages may leave the train and complete the journey by car to BERLIN. Neither the Führerzug nor von Ribbentrop's special stops at FREILASSING Junction. The speed of the Führerzug varies from 90-120 kilometres p.h., 100 km. p.h. being the average maximum.

On the journey from BERLIN to SALZBURG the two steam locomotives are changed for electric locomotives at HALLE. During the winter months, however, one electric and one steam locomotive are used instead of two electric locomotives. The locomotives are changed again either at RODENKIRCHEN or at PROSTZELLA and again at NUREMBERG or REGENSBURG. A further change may also be made at LANDSHUT. The only tunnel on this route is the short tunnel 2.7 km. north of ROHRBACH, disregarding the tunnel just outside BERCHTESGADEN.

2. To the west. (MANNHEIM).

The route after passing through FREILASSING Junction followed by the Führerzug in this case is believed to be as follows: MUNICH, AUGSBURG, ULM, STUTTGART, HEIDELBERG, MANNHEIM. The track is electric as far as Stuttgart.

The only tunnels on this line are at Stuttgart, viz. one tunnel 340 m. long in the BAD CANSTATT-STUTTGARTER HAUPTBAHNHOF section (actually in the town) and another 700 m. long between STUTTGART-NORD and STUTTGART-Feuerbach on the other side of the town.

E. Possibilities of action in connection with the Führerzug.

It is evident from the foregoing notes that the information available regarding the Führerzug and its movements is nothing like so complete or precise as the information given for the Berchtesgaden projects (in Part I). The expediency of a final check-up on the spot by the operatives or their leader before carrying out the selected project in this case is stressed.

The following two addresses in the Salzburg district might prove useful hide-outs (being places at which one can stay and no questions asked): Gasthof MEYER at HOF (a small township 8 miles east of Salzburg) and Ainringsweg 13, Salzburg-GNEIS 2.

Actions in connection with the Führerzug are outlined below.

1. At the Schloss KLESSHEIM sidings.

Fig.1 and Fig.61 (below) show the route from the Berghof via Schloss Klessheim to the sidings and the immediate approaches to these sidings. It is not known which route the Kolonne takes after leaving or passing the Schloss.

If the left-hand fork is taken, the road runs into the sidings alongside the wood north of the Schloss. Though apparently thick enough in summer, this wood might not afford a great deal of cover in winter, since its trees are mostly of the deciduous type. It should nevertheless afford adequate cover for a sniper or a PIAT party located at the edge of the wood (and road) opposite the building at the N.W. end of the sidings, as well as a good shot (under 100 yards) at Hitler as he descended from his car.

Should the Kolonne take the right-hand fork, or proceed direct along the Autobahn without touching Schloss Klessheim, the point at which Hitler would probably leave his car is in the vicinity of the building at the S.E. end of the sidings - a distance of well over 300 yards from the wood and accordingly out of sniper's range, though probably within range of a PIAT gun.

It is true that the wood is uncomfortably close to Schloss Klessheim and the Führerbegleitbataillon.

Fig.61. Schloss Klessheim and its sidings.

Any attempt as outlined under 2. below to interfere with the train at the Klessheim sidings would be out of the question since apart from the fact that Klessheim is a private station and not open to the public, the train is guarded and serviced+ (washed) by personnel of the Begleitbataillon.

2. At Salzburg railway station.

Fig.62 and 63 show the station and sidings at Salzburg. Hitler's train is still, it is believed, occasionally serviced at Salzburg station where it was reported in July 1944 as occupying the position shown in Fig.62 (alongside v. Ribbentrop's train).

Only the sides of the coaches of special trains are washed; the tops of the coaches, it would appear, are not cleaned. This job is performed by 6 French workers (female) dressed in black overalls (knee length, buttoned) without distinguishing badge. Interference with the drinking and cooking water is the only clandestine means which offers itself. The only point at which the water can be "doctored" is the tank above the kitchen of the MITROPA dining car, since it appears quite definite that water trolley wagons are not used (as in this country) for taking on drinking water

Whether or not it would be possible for one of these cleaners to get at the tank immediately above the kitchen of the MITROPA dining car (Fig.64) during the final wash that special trains are given shortly before proceeding on a journey is doubtful. They are apparently approachable (see C. above) and an attempt to suborn one of them might be worth while.

It might be possible for an operative to introduce the medium at night,x provided the guards, as in the case of v. Ribbentrop's train, consisted of only a couple of Bahnpolizei, specially if the latter's attention could be diverted for the necessary time by a second operative. (The lighting at Salzburg station is described as extremely poor).

The medium which is described in Appendix V would best be introduced into the tank in the form of a strong solution which the jolting of the train as soon as it got into motion would tend to distribute evenly in the water.

The capacity of the tank in question is 540 litres, i.e. about 120 gallons. The quantity of medium necessary to obtain the desired results is about 768 grams. and would weigh somewhat under 2 lbs.

+ It is not known whether water for drinking and cooking purposes can be taken in at the Klessheim sidings or whether the train has to be taken to Salzburg for this purpose.

x The night before the train was due to leave.

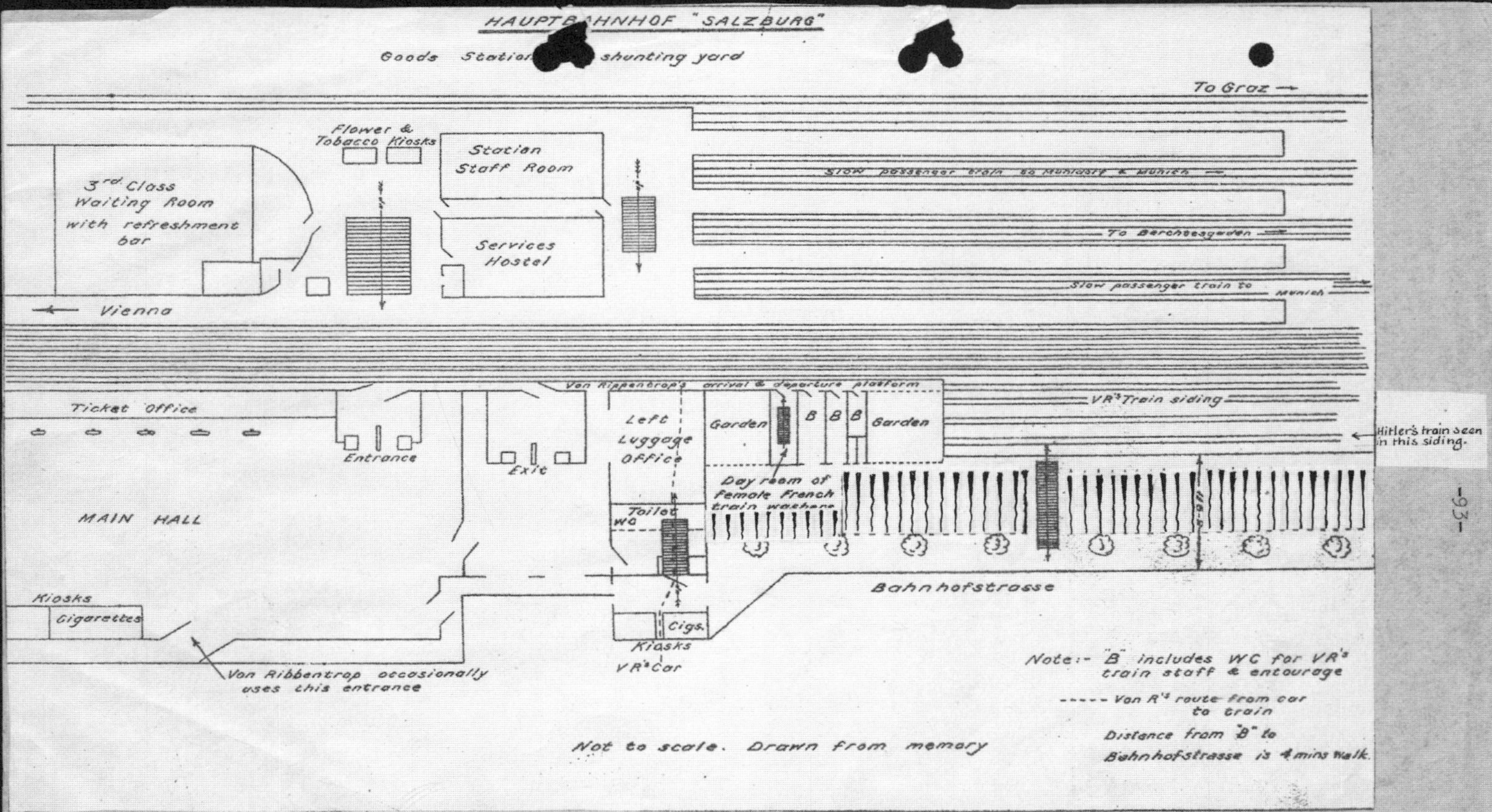

Fig.62. Salzburg main railway station and sidings used by the Sonderzüge (Party specials).

There is no page 101 in the Operation FOXLEY folder

Fig. 63

LEGEND.

1. Cafe LOHR.
2. PLATZKELLER.
3. NEUE STAATSBRÜCKE.
4. ÖSTERR HOF.
5. LANDESTHEATER.
6. MIRABELLKASINO.
7. LAZARETT.
8. Cafe FUENFHAUS.
9. Cafe PITTER.
10. Cafe BURGUND.
11. GEN. KDO. (HOTEL EUROP).
12. BAHNHOF.
13. ANDRE KIRCHE.

-95-

Fig. 64. MITROPA dining car similar to that used on the Führerzug and the Party specials.

Note: The tank for drinking and cooking water is housed above the kitchen.

3. En route.

From the notes given under B.2 (Protection of the Führerzug) above, the most favourable point for derailing and destroying Hitler's train is a tunnel.[+] In Germany not only is the track itself relatively free from Bahnpolizei or military patrols compared with occupied territory where guards are stationed in some cases every 100-200 yards (as was the case in the Ukraine, for example), but neither bridges nor tunnels are so heavily guarded as in occupied territory (see Fig.65).

Moreover now that every active man is serving at the front, the category of Landesschützen personnel (never very high) is likely in future to be even lower than before. A sabotage party disguised as Bahnpolizei with one member in mufti (as Gestapo man), or as Landesschützen would not arouse the suspicion of the guards, and should be able to "take over", lay their charges as shown in Appendix IV and destroy the train in the tunnel.

Another means of approach in laying charges in longer tunnels, as at Stuttgart for example, would be to enter the tunnel by the ventilation shaft, though this might involve cutting through the ventilation grating (with a blow lamp).

In either case it would be necessary to have an operative (with W/T set) further up the line on which the Führerzug was passing, in order to warn the sabotage party of the train's approach.

An attempt might also be made to derail the train as it passed through a station, by throwing under its wheels a suitcase filled with explosive. For this the train would have to be passing on a track adjacent to the platform on which the operative was standing or only one track removed therefrom, and the operative be prepared to take the consequences.

It is probable that suitable operatives for either of the schemes outlined above would be available among German or Austrian Ps/W. with a sufficiently strong hatred for Hitler.

[+] Should it be found on closer investigation that signal boxes on routes taken by the Führerzug in Germany are only lightly guarded, then the same means (impersonation) as that described for tunnels might be employed here too.

Derailment of Hitler's train when travelling at speed by switching it into a siding, say, has the advantage of requiring no explosion charges.

Fig. 65.

September, 1944

APPENDIX I - Hitler's Cars.

The cars in which Hitler is driven are always of Mercedes make. No photograph is available of the latest armoured 6-seater Mercedes-Nürburg type reported to have windscreens and sidescreens of bullet-proof glass 2 ins. thick. They are, however, otherside similar to the Mercedes 4 or 6 wheeled touring cars shown in Figs.67-73 and Figs.76-78 below.

The black Mercedes limousine shown in Figs.74 and 75 is, however, employed in very cold weather, and Hitler is reported to have made considerable use of this type of car in Russia.

Number plates are useless as a means of identifying the Führer's car, the Nationalstandard (Fig.66) carried on the right-hand mudguard + being the surest means of identification: As the photographs show, it is Hitler's practice to sit beside his driver (Sturmbannführer KEMKA) in the leading car, unless accompanied by any important foreign personages like Mussolini or the Regent HORTHY (see Fig.77) when he sits in the back seat.

Hitler's car is however usually the second car in the Kolonne when driving from the Berghof to Schloss Klessheim sidings.

Fig.66.

+ Fig.66 shows it on the left-hand mudguard. This particular photo was taken of Mussolini's car, which bore on the right-hand mudguard the Fascist emblem (lictor's rods).

Fig.67. Hitler at the opening of the Nazi Party Congress, Nuremburg.

Sturmbannführer KEMKA, Hitler's driver, is seated at the Führer's side.

Fig.68. Hitler at Memel.
The seated figure immediately behind Hitler is KRAUSE, once Hitler's valet, and now an officer of the Begleitkommando.

Fig. 69. Hitler at Nuremberg Rally.
Behind Hitler (to his right) KRAUSE and (to his left) Brigadeführer SCHAUB.

Fig. 70. Another photograph of Hitler in his car (Nuremberg Rally).

KRAUSE   ENGELS (a German Wehrmacht (Heer) adjutant)

SCHMUNDT

Fig.71. Hitler in 6-wheeled Mercedes touring car.
Note: army number plates on this car. and side screen.

Fig.72. Hitler in armoured 6-wheeled Mercedes touring car.

Note: army number plate.

Fig.73. Hitler entering his car after inspecting guard of honour at Anhalter Bahnhof on his return from France, 1940.

SCHULZ side-de-camp to Hitler, recently killed in Normandy and replaced as ADC by the

Fig. 74. Front view of Hitler's black Mercedes limousine.

Fig.75. Side of Hitler's black Mercedes limousine.

Hitler is seen leaving the British Embassy in Berlin after the conclusion of the talks with Mr. Eden and Sir John Simon in March 1935.

Fig.76. The Kolonne with Hitler in leading car alongside his driver KEMKA.

115

Fig. 77. The Kolonne with Hitler in back seat alongside HORTHY, the Regent of Hungary.

Fig. 78. The Kolonne with Hitler in leading car driving from the Anhalter Bahnhof to the Reichskanzlei on Hitler's return to Berlin from France July 1940.
Note: rosestrewn street.

APPENDIX II - SCHLOSS KLESSHEIM.

Schloss KLESSHEIM (Fig.79) is an 18th century mansion, built in the classical style and set in formal gardens; it is approached by a conspicuous double drive, entered through an elaborate brick wall gateway. To the south of the mansion, at a short distance, is a group of buildings which includes stables. To the north, between the house and the railway line lies a wood.

There are searchlight and light Flak positions in the immediate vicinity of the Schloss, 1000 yards north-east of which run railway sidings.

Schloss KLESSHEIM was first mentioned as Führerhauptquartier in January 1944. Whilst the Russian front held and Russia was the principal theatre of operations Führerhauptquartier (both at VINNITSA and ZHITOMIR) included the field headquarters of the Oberkommando der Wehrmacht. These headquarters were subsequently withdrawn with the advance of the Russian armies in Poland to RASTENBERG (East Prussia) - the former location of FHQ at the commencement of the Russian campaign. Although the furthest point to which the Russians have pressed the Germans back on the frontier of East Prussia is no more than 100 km. from RASTENBERG, this place is still apparently OKW for the Eastern front. OKW - Western front is probably located at MUNSINGEN near STUTTGART.

Fig.79.

The impossibility of accommodating the whole of FHQ, including the field headquarters of the OKW in this building is clearly indicated in the plan of Schloss Klessheim given in Fig.80. It is probable that, apart from its use for reception purposes it only accommodates that part of OKW which includes the WEHRMACHTFÜHRUNGSTAB (W.F.St.) or Armed Forces Operations Staff. At FHQ RASTENBERG W.F.St. totalled about 35 officers under JODL and WARLIMONT.

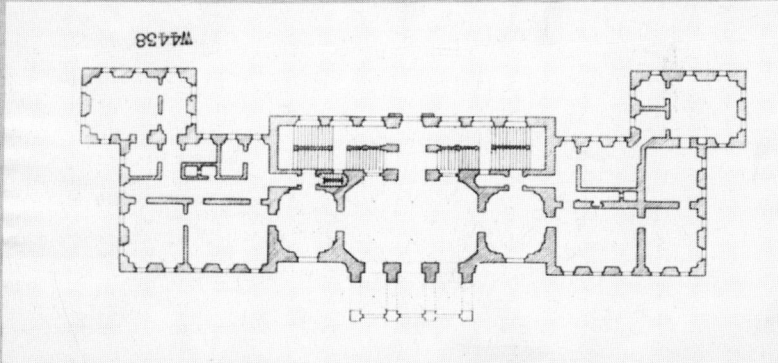

Fig.80.

It may also house that part of the Führerbegleitbataillon which is stationed at Schloss Klessheim (to protect this FHQ and the adjacent sidings, including the Führerzug).

The Führerbegleitbataillon consists of 4-6 companies. These include A.A. company, heavy company with armoured cars, and 2-4 motorised guard (Wach) companies. Its estimated strength is 1250. It is probable that the battalion has been split up and distributed among the various FHQs.

+ On such occasions as the Führer's birthday, e.g. 20th s April, 1944, when Hitler is reported to have received 200 generals at Schloss KLESSHEIM.

APPENDIX III - FOREIGN WORKERS IN SALZBURG AND DISTRICT.

The total number of foreign workers in the seven Austrian Gaue is estimated at 1,200,000 of whom probably about 100,000-150,000 are employed in and around Salzburg.

Whereas the more favoured foreign workers, e.g. French and Italians, were once frequently able to live in private lodgings, the influx into Salzburg and other Austrain towns of refugees from bombed German cities has caused this privilege to be withdrawn, and a decree of the local Gauleiter[+] of 18/1/1944 forbade hotel-keepers and other landlords to house male foreign workers or to renew the leases of rooms let to foreign tenants. Except in the case of domestic servants, workers in hotels, restaurants, and cafes, and labourers on isolated farms, it is likely that all foreign workers are now housed in communal camps (Gemeinschaftslager) in the Salzburg area.

Ostarbeiter i.e. Russian and Ukrainian deportees and Ps/W constitute the great majority of foreign workers in Salzburg and district (HALLEIN for example). They include a large proportion of females, many of whom are employed as domestics in Salzburg itself. Others are employed on the railways as carriage cleaners, as at BERCHTESGADEN station for example. Like the Poles, they can be distinguished from other foreign workers by the badge they wear on the left breast of their overalls (Fig.81).

Fig.81.

Only second in number to the Ostarbeiter are the Poles, of whom about 15,000 are employed in Salzburg and its immediate vicinity (out of an estimated total of Poles in the whole of Austria of 200,000). Apart from agriculture and road construction, Poles in the Salzburg area are employed in textile mills, salt works, hydro-electric plants and on the railways, Polish workers being found at Salzburg station [x] as well as at BERCHTESGADEN station. Here Polish women are employed as carriage cleaners. Like the Ostarbeiter, the Poles are housed in camps where they are also fed separately from other inmates. Poles (and Ostarbeiter) may enter cafes but are not allowed to speak to Germans. They wear the badge shown in Fig.82 on the left breast of their overalls.

[+] Dr. SCHREL, Reichsstatthalter and Gauleiter, SALZBURG. Other notabilities at Salzburg: Gen. RINGEL, GOC Wehrkreis XVIII
SS Obersturmführer TRAUT i/c SD Abschnitt, Salzburg.

[x] On night of 12/11/44 a French worker saw 3 Polish workers break off the seals of a Reichspostwagen. Clothes obtained in earlier thefts were found in their lodgings (Salzburger Zeitung 18/11/4).

Fig.82.

The next most numerous nationality amongst foreign workers is the French. These include deportees and Ps/W (prisonniers de guerre transformes). They enjoy much better treatment than Ostarbeiter or Poles and are allowed out at night until 10 or 11 o/c. In addition to the establishment of welfare offices (Landesbauernschaft, Salzburg), the Nussdorferbar in the Franz-Josef Strasse was recently turned over to the French as a "foyer". Frenchmen (and women) are employed at Salzburg railway station, where the latter are entrusted with the washing of the Party's special trains.

Czech foreign workers are also to be found in Salzburg and district, a few being employed at Salzburg railway station.[+] There are two Czech camps on the OBERSALZBERG, almost within stone's throw of Hitler's residence.

Considerable numbers of Italian workers have been employed at one time or another as railwaymen, waiters, and in factories, etc. Like the French they receive favoured treatment.

Other nationalities found among the foreign worker population include Croats, Serbs (at HALLEIN), Bulgarians, Greeks, etc.

According to Russian sources, many foreign workers in Austria have fled from their places of employment and formed themselves into guerilla bands. Baldur v. SCHIRACH, the Gauleiter for Austria, is reported to have issued orders in July 1944 to every member of the Nazi Party "to hunt out the thousands of foreign workers who have joined the guerillas".

+ Three Czechs and a Croat employed as workers at Salzburg railway station were sentenced to 2-4 years imprisonment for theft (Salzburger Zeitung 13/2/44).

APPENDIX IV - ATTEMPT IN WEST PRUSSIA TO BLOW UP THE FUHRERZUG.

The attempt was made in the autumn of 1941 on the railway between FREIDORF and SCHWARZWASSER by Polish saboteurs, whose orders, in point of fact, were to derail any fast train. It was therefore purely a matter of chance that the opportunity of destroying the Führer in his train presented itself. The detachment did, it is true, receive warning by radio from their HQ in West Prussia of the train's departure from KÖNIGSBERG shortly after it had left. At that time Polish saboteurs were organised in detachments, every Kreis (district) having its detachment of 12 men, viz. wireless operator, six men for laying charges etc. and five men for local protection. Arms included machine pistols and revolvers. Communication was by short wave radio and each detachment had a set. This set was used not only for communicating with HQ and other detachments, but also for firing the charge. For some undisclosed reason the Führerzug stopped at a neighbouring station and another train was let through.

The several 2 kg. charges were laid some 20-30 mins. before the train was timed to pass, and were detonated by a current controlled by a receiving set which received the impress over the air from a short wave transmitter approximately 400 metres away from the line.

The resulting explosion is described as devasting, 430 Germans being killed and the line blocked for two days. The method of securing the charges to the rail and firing them is illustrated in Figs.83a,b and c below.

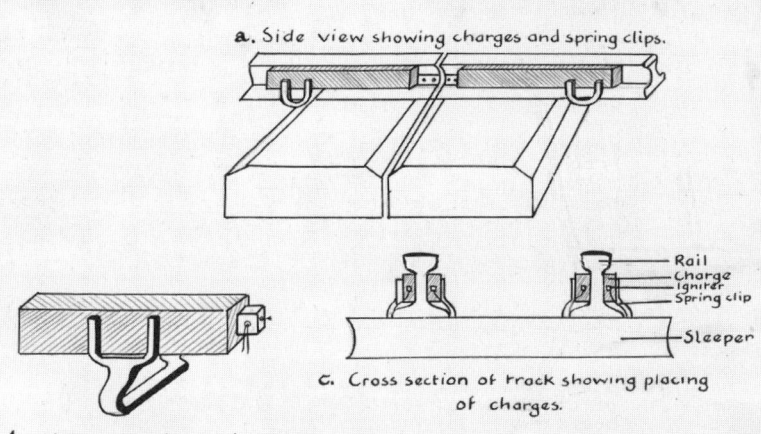

Figs.83a,b and c.

APPENDIX V - "I" AS THE CLANDESTINE MEANS.

(see Part II - E).

"I" has been chosen as the most suitable medium, since its effect is not immediate like that of "R" or "F". In fact, taken in sufficiently small doses its symptons may not appear before 6 or 7 days. Under such circumstances there is no antidote.

Though a lethal dose (2 grams. in 2½ pints) taken at one and the same time might produce symptons (colic) the same day, the same quantity taken in cupfuls at a time in the morning, (Tea at breakfast) and the evening (coffee after dinner), would not occasion such symptons possibly for a day or two.

The delayed action of this medium is its chief advantage since it affords the best chance of the intended victim (Hitler) taking the necessary lethal quantity before suspicion has been aroused though any member of his entourage or of the train staff who has likewise taken beverages containing "I" may fall suddenly ill.

The characteristics of "I" are as follows:-

1. It is tasteless and odourless.

2. Neither hard nor soft water is visibly affected by the addition of one lethal dose (2 grams. to 2½ pints).

3. Black coffee treated with "I" in the same ratio indicates no perceptible change in appearance. Nor would the addition of milk make any immediate difference in the appearance of the beverage.

4. Tea (with milk) treated as above shows no detectable change, but without milk it immediately becomes opalescent and in the course of an hour or so becomes quite turbid and deposits a brown sediment.

5. Fruit such as apples and prunes, and vegetables (cabbage), stewed or boiled in water containing one lethal dose of "I" (2 grams.) to 2½ pints of water shows no abnormality compared with the same materials boiled in ordinary tap water. Though only insignificant quantities of "I" would be absorbed by the fruit or vegetable, the juice would be lethal.

6. The addition of "I" at the rate of one lethal dose to ½ pint of beer causes no alteration whatever in appearance.

7. Wines and spirits treated with "I" become turbid or cloudy at once and gradually deposit a dark brown sediment.

x x x x x x x x x x

Hitler, according to reliable information, is a tea addict. He always drinks it with milk. Since the milk is poured first into the cup, it is unlikely that the tea's opalescence (see 4. above) would be noticed as it came from the teapot.

Hitler is said to be extremely fond of apple juice.

The reports that he drinks enormous quantities of black coffee, which have appeared in the popular press from time to time, are denied by P/W who was body-servant to Hitler from 1936 to 1940, although a dining car attendant from von Ribbentrop's train declares this is not so and that he personally served the Führer with coffee (and milk) at the Berghof. Hitler may well have formed the habit in the course of the war.

Apart from such table waters as FACHINGER and APOLINARIS the only other beverage Hitler takes is his "near beer". This beer is said to be a special product of the HOLZKIRCHEN brewery, Munich, whose lorry makes a delivery once a month to the Berghof. (It is difficult to see how this beer could be treated outside the brewery, i.e. before bottling).

Notes

1 "We Are Not Mad, Nor Is This a Joke"

1 The National Archives (hereafter TNA), HS 6/623: Special Operations Executive: Western Europe, "Politics: operation FOXLEY: plan to liquidate Hitler and/or his satellites", p. 69.
2 The identity of the French officer has never been revealed.
3 HS 6/623, p. 64.
4 Ibid., p. 67. Other than this passing reference to a 1941 plan – which was never attempted – little seems to be known about this early SOE decision to kill Hitler, and it seems to have had no results.
5 Schmitt, Michael N., "State-Sponsored Assassination in International and Domestic Law", *Yale Journal of International Law*, 17:609, 1992, 614.

2 Man Hunt

1 Hoffmann, Peter, *Hitler's Personal Security* (London: Macmillan Press Ltd, 1979), p. 24.
2 Tim Newark, "Operation Foxley: British Sniping and the Hunt for Hitler", in John L. Plaster, et al., *The Sniper Anthology: Snipers of the Second World War* (London: Frontline Books, 2012), p. 62.

3 TNA, HS 6/624: Special Operations Executive: Western Europe, "Operation FOXLEY", p. 72. FHQ means Führer Headquarters.
4 Mauser company website: www.mauser.com/en.html.
5 Foot, M.R.D., *SOE: An Outline History of the Special Operations Executive 1940–46* (London: British Broadcasting Corporation, 1984), p. 78.
6 Ibid. Yes, Foot refers to yards and metres in the same sentence.

3 The Unlikely Assassin

1 Foot, *SOE*, p. 205.
2 Howarth, Patrick, *Undercover: The Men and Women of the SOE* (London: Phoenix Press, 1980). p. 38. There is a short biography of Alfgar Hesketh-Prichard in John Walter's *Sniper Encyclopaedia*.
3 Howarth, p. 46.
4 Newark, p. 66.
5 TNA, HS 9/124/6: Special Operations Executive: Personnel Files: "Edmund Hailey BENNETT – born 10.05.1919".
6 Rigden, Denis, *Kill the Führer: Section X and Operation Foxley* (Stroud: History Press, 1999), p. 86.
7 Foot, *SOE*, p. 206.
8 Rigden, p. 87.
9 Ibid., p. 88.
10 Ibid. The actual memo raising these issues is to be found in TNA, HS 6/625: Special Operations Executive: Western Europe, "Operation FOXLEY", p. 6.
11 Ibid.
12 Ibid., p. 88.
13 Moorhouse, Roger, *Killing Hitler: The Third Reich and the Plots to Kill the Führer* (London: Vintage Books, 2007), pp. 168–169.
14 Mark Seaman described Bennett as "an officer who may have been in line for the task, or at least one aspect of it" in *Operation Foxley: The British Plan to Kill Hitler*, introduction by Mark Seaman, with a foreword by Ian Kershaw (London: Public Record Office, 1998), p. 24.
15 Millar, Stuart, "He Was Just a Backroom Boy … Then They Chose Him to Kill the Führer", *Guardian*, 25 July 1998.

Notes

16 HS 9/124/6.
17 Hulme, Charlie, "Edmund Harley Bennett and Operation Foxley", A Davenport history feature, www.davenportstation.org.uk/bennett.html.
18 Millar.

4 The Perfect Murder

1 Swanson, Peter, "Sixteen of the Most Perfect Murders in Crime Fiction", Crime Reads, 6 March 2020, https://crimereads.com/sixteen-of-the-most-perfect-murders-in-crime-fiction/.
2 Christie, Agatha. *The Pale Horse* (London: Agatha Christie Ltd/Planet Three, 2001), p. 240.
3 Emsley, John, *Elements of Murder* (Oxford: Oxford University Press, 2005), pp. 324–325.
4 Evans, Rob, "The Past Porton Down Can't Hide", *Guardian*, 6 May 2004. www.theguardian.com/science/2004/may/06/science.research.
5 See www.gov.uk/government/news/the-truth-about-porton-down.
6 HS 6/624, p. 95,
7 Ibid., p. 121.
8 Ibid.
9 In typical English style, the dossier is inconsistent, using both metric and imperial measures, even in the same sentence.
10 Ibid., p. 122.
11 Emsley, pp. 324–325.
12 Ibid., p. 332.
13 Ibid., pp. 331–332.
14 Ibid., p. 337.
15 He was also head of the Medical Research Council's Bacteriological Metabolic Unit in the 1930s and leader of the British biological warfare team. A Fellow of the Royal Society, awarded an OBE, he was also a recipient of the Copley Medal. Three portraits of him hang in London's National Portrait Gallery.
16 Everett was part of the SOE scientific team, and was awarded an MBE in 1945 for his efforts.

17 Boyce, Frederick and Douglass Everett, *SOE: The Scientific Secrets* (Stroud: History Press, 2003), p. 84.
18 Harris, Robert, and Jeremy Paxman, *A Higher Form of Killing: The Secret History of Gas and Germ Warfare* (London: Chatto & Windus, 1982), p. 89.
19 Ibid., p. 95.
20 Foot, *SOE*, p. 200.
21 Tatu, Laurent, Wolfgang Jost and Julien Bogousslavsky, "The Botulinum Toxin Legend of Reinhard Heydrich's Death: The End of 'Himmler's Brain'", *Neurology*, 89, 2017, 84–87, https://medicinainternaelsalvador.com/wp-content/uploads/2017/08/Historia-del-desarrollo-bioterrorismo-.pdf.

5   The Manchurian Candidate

1 HS 6/623, p. 56.
2 Ibid., p. 33. I have not been able to identify the "American Officer stationed in Ireland" that Manderstam refers to.
3 Rigden, pp. 61–62.
4 Manderstam, Major L.H. with Roy Heron, *From the Red Army to SOE* (London: William Kimber, 1985), p. 113.
5 Cooper, Dick, *Adventures of a Secret Agent* (Maidstone: Mann, 1973), p. 88. The author acknowledges with thanks the help of Pat Hews, Dick Cooper's daughter, in locating this text.
6 Seaman, in *Operation Foxley*, p. 27.
7 Rigden, p. 61.
8 Ibid., p. 65. Rigden quoted from doctors' reports on Hess, but nowhere mentioned Hess' strong views on hypnosis, which are relevant.
9 Moorhouse, p. 168.
10 "The Secret Plan to Kill Hitler", BBC News, 23 July 1998, http://news.bbc.co.uk/1/hi/uk/137570.stm.
11 Marks, John, *The Search for the "Manchurian Candidate": The CIA and Mind Control* (New York: Norton, 1991), p. 133.
12 Condon, Richard, *The Manchurian Candidate* (London: Orion, 2004), p. 45.
13 Ibid.

Notes

14 Andrew Salter cited a 1933 article which appeared in the *American Journal of Diseases of Children.* Salter, Andrew, *What is Hypnosis? Studies in Auto and Hetero Conditioning* (London: Athenaeum Press, 1950), p. 27.
15 Wells, Wesley Raymond, "Experiments in the Hypnotic Production of Crime", *Journal of Psychology*, 11:1, 1941, 63–102, DOI: 10.1080/00223980.1941.9917019.
16 Brenman, Margaret, "Experiments in the Hypnotic Production of Anti-Social and Self-Injurious Behavior", *Psychiatry*, 5:1, 1942, 49–61, DOI: 10.1080/00332747.1942.11022380.
17 Rees, J.R. (ed.), *The Case of Rudolf Hess: A Problem in Diagnosis and Forensic Psychiatry* (London: William Heinemann, 1947), p. ix.
18 Ibid., p. 53.
19 Ibid., pp. 114–115.
20 Ibid., p. 71.
21 Ibid., p. 72.
22 The MKULTRA programme was approved by CIA director Allen Dulles on 13 April 1953. The cryptonym probably had no specific meaning, though the MK meant it was linked to a CIA division known as the Technical Services Staff (TSS).
23 The story of Sirhan as a possible real-life "Manchurian candidate" is told in Tim Tate and Brad Johnson, *The Assassination of Robert F. Kennedy: Crime Conspiracy and Cover-Up – A New Investigation* (London: Thistle Books, 2018). One of the stranger parts of the Sirhan story is that Robert Kennedy's friend, who drove the Senator to the hotel in Los Angeles where he met his death, and who was waiting to take him home, was John Frankenheimer, the director of *The Manchurian Candidate.*
24 "The Assassin", *Derren Brown: The Experiments*, Objective Productions, 2011, television.
25 Email to the author, 23 November 2020.
26 Email to the author, 24 November 2020.
27 Martin S. Taylor's website is at www.hypnotism.co.uk.
28 Brown, Derren, *Tricks of the Mind* (London: Channel 4 Books, 2006), pp. 8–9.

29 Interview with Martin S. Taylor, 28 October 2020.

6 "Peace on Earth to All Men of Good Will"
1 HS 6/625, p. 7.
2 Foot, *SOE*, p. 39.

7 Combined Operation
1 HS 6/623, p. 9.
2 Moorhouse, p. 172.

8 Stalin's "Hitler Scheme"
1 Werner, Ruth [Ursula Kuczynski], *Sonya's Report*, translated by Renate Simpson (London: Chatto & Windus, 1991), p. 194.
2 Macintyre, Ben, *Agent Sonya: Lover, Mother, Soldier, Spy* (London: Viking, 2020), p. 147.
3 Werner, p. 194.
4 Foote, Alexander, *Handbook for Spies* (London: Museum Press Limited, 1964), p. 26.
5 Ibid., p. 29.
6 Ibid., p. 31.
7 MacIntyre, p. 164.
8 Foote, p. 31.
9 Ibid., p. 32.
10 Ibid.
11 Ibid.
12 Ibid., p. 33.
13 Ibid., p. 35.
14 Werner, p. 200.
15 Moorhouse, p. 115.
16 Moorhouse, p. 131.
17 Ibid., p. 138.
18 Ibid., p. 141.

9 "Professor Moriarty"
1 Lovell, Stanley P., *Of Spies and Stratagems* (Englewood Cliffs: Prentice-Hall, 1963), p. 17.

2 Kean, Sam, "The Bizarre Ways America's First Spy Agency Tried to Overthrow Hitler", *The Atlantic*, 9 July 2019.
3 Lovell, p. 81.
4 Ibid.
5 Ibid.
6 Ibid., p. 82.
7 Ibid., p. 83.
8 Ibid., p. 84.
9 Langer, Walter C., *A Psychological Analysis of Adolf Hitler: His Life and Legend* (AllAboutPsychology.com, 2011, Kindle edition), p. 121.
10 Ibid., p. 123.
11 Ibid., p. 116.
12 Ibid., p. 151.
13 Lovell, p. 85.
14 Alois Schicklgruber was Hitler's father; he changed the family name to Hitler before Adolf was born.
15 Lovell, p. 89.
16 Marks, p. 20.
17 Ibid.
18 Lovell, p. 90.
19 Macintyre, p. 275.

Conclusion

1 Ford, Franklin L., *Political Murder: From Tyrannicide to Terrorism* (Cambridge: Harvard University Press, 1985), p. 280.
2 Moorhouse, p. 169.

Bibliography

National Archives
Special Operations Executive: Western Europe
  HS 6/623: "Politics: operation FOXLEY: plan to liquidate Hitler and/or his satellites"
  HS 6/624: "Operation FOXLEY"
  HS 6/625: "Operation FOXLEY"
  HS 6/626: "Little Foxleys"
Special Operations Executive: Personnel Files
  HS 9/124/6: "Edmund Hailey BENNETT – born 10.05.1919"

Articles
Brenman, Margaret, "Experiments in the Hypnotic Production of Anti-Social and Self-Injurious Behavior", *Psychiatry*, 5:1, 1942, 49-61, DOI: 10.1080/00332747.1942.11022380.
Hulme, Charlie, "Edmund Harley Bennett and Operation Foxley", A Davenport history feature, www.davenportstation.org.uk/bennett.html.
Humphries, Conor, "Stalin Blocked Attempts to Kill Hitler: General", Reuters, 25 May 2010.
Kean, Sam, "The Bizarre Ways America's First Spy Agency Tried to Overthrow Hitler", *The Atlantic*, 9 July 2019.

Millar, Stuart, "He was Just a Backroom Boy ... Then They Chose Him to Kill the Führer", *Guardian*, 25 July 1998.

Schmitt, Michael N., "State-Sponsored Assassination in International and Domestic Law," *Yale Journal of International Law*, 17:609, 1992.

Tatu, Laurent, Wolfgang Jost and Julien Bogousslavsky, "The Botulinum Toxin Legend of Reinhard Heydrich's Death: The End of 'Himmler's Brain'", *Neurology*, 89, 2017, 84–87, https://medicinainternaelsalvador.com/wp-content/uploads/2017/08/Historia-del-desarrollo-bioterrorismo-.pdf.

Wells, Wesley Raymond, "Experiments in the Hypnotic Production of Crime", *Journal of Psychology*, 11:1, 1941, 63–102.

Books

Boyce, Frederick and Douglass Everett, *SOE: The Scientific Secrets* (Stroud: History Press, 2003).

Brown, Derren, *Tricks of the Mind* (London: Channel 4 Books, 2006).

Christie, Agatha. *The Pale Horse* (London: Agatha Christie Ltd/Planet Three, 2001).

Condon, Richard, *The Manchurian Candidate* (London: Orion, 2004).

Cooper, Dick, *Adventures of a Secret Agent* (Maidstone: Mann, 1973).

Emsley, John, *Elements of Murder* (Oxford: Oxford University Press, 2005) .

Felton, Mark, *Guarding Hitler: The Secret World of the Führer* (Barnsley: Pen & Sword, 2020).

Foot, M.R.D., *Memories of an SOE Historian* (Barnsley: Pen & Sword, 2008).

Foot, M.R.D., *SOE: An Outline History of the Special Operations Executive 1940–46* (London: British Broadcasting Corporation, 1984).

Foote, Alexander, *Handbook for Spies* (London: Museum Press Limited, 1964).

Ford, Franklin L., *Political Murder: From Tyrannicide to Terrorism* (Cambridge: Harvard University Press, 1985).

Bibliography

Harper, David, *Your Complete Guide to Berchtesgaden* (Berchtesgaden: D. Harper & Ch. Dundas-Harper, Gdbr., 1997).

Harris, Robert, and Jeremy Paxman, *A Higher Form of Killing: The Secret History of Gas and Germ Warfare* (London: Chatto & Windus, 1982).

Hoffmann, Peter, *Hitler's Personal Security* (London: Macmillan Press, 1979).

Household, Geoffrey, *Rogue Male* (London: Chatto & Windus, 1939).

Household, Geoffrey, *Against the Wind* (London: Michael Joseph, 1958).

Household, Geoffrey, *Rogue Justice* (London: Joseph, 1982).

Howarth, Patrick, *Undercover: The Men and Women of the SOE* (London: Phoenix Press, 1980).

Langer, Walter C., *A Psychological Analysis of Adolf Hitler: His Life and Legend* (AllAboutPsychology.com, 2011, Kindle edition).

Lovell, Stanley P., *Of Spies and Stratagems* (Englewood Cliffs: Prentice-Hall, 1963).

Macintyre, Ben, *Agent Sonya: Lover, Mother, Soldier, Spy* (London: Viking, 2020).

Manderstam, Major L.H. with Roy Heron, *From the Red Army to SOE* (London: William Kimber, 1985).

Marcus, Greil, *The Manchurian Candidate* (London: British Film Institute, 2002).

Marks, John, *The Search for the "Manchurian Candidate": The CIA and Mind Control* (New York: Norton, 1991).

Moorhouse, Roger, *Killing Hitler: The Third Reich and the Plots to Kill the Führer* (London: Vintage Books, 2007).

Operation Foxley: The British Plan to Kill Hitler, introduction by Mark Seaman, foreword by Ian Kershaw (London: Public Record Office, 1998).

Plaster, John L., et al., *The Sniper Anthology: Snipers of the Second World War* (London: Frontline Books, 2012).

Rees, J.R. (ed.), *The Case of Rudolf Hess: A Problem in Diagnosis and Forensic Psychiatry* (London: William Heinemann, 1947).

Rigden, Denis, *Kill the Führer: Section X and Operation Foxley* (Stroud: History Press, 1999).

Salter, Andrew, *What is Hypnosis? Studies in Auto and Hetero Conditioning* (London: Athenaeum Press, 1950).

Tate, Tim and Brad Johnson, *The Assassination of Robert F. Kennedy: Crime Conspiracy and Cover-Up – A New Investigation* (London: Thistle Publishing, 2018).

Waldern, Geoffrey R., *Hitler's Berchtesgaden: A Guide to Third Reich Sites in the Berchtesgaden and Obersalzberg Area* (Stroud: Fonthill Media, 2014).

Walter, John, *The Sniper Encyclopaedia: An A-Z Guide to World Sniping* (London: Greenhill Books, 2019).

Werner, Ruth [Ursula Kuczynski], *Sonya's Report*, translated by Renate Simpson (London: Chatto & Windus, 1991).

Wilson, James, *Hitler's Alpine Retreat* (Barnsley: Pen & Sword Military, 2005).

Movies and Television

Man Hunt, dir. Fritz Lang. Twentieth Century Fox, 1941, film.

"Operation Foxley – Mission: Liquidate Hitler (WWII Documentary)", World at War, dir. Guilain Depardieu, 2016, www.youtube.com/watch?v=1tQWj3ggfUI

Rogue Male, dir. Clive Donner, BBC, 1976, film.

"The Assassin", *Derren Brown: The Experiments*. Objective Productions, 2011, television.

Acknowledgements

This book could not have been written without the help of many individuals who answered my questions, provided me with documents, or read over early drafts of what I had written.

I'd like to thank Cindy Berman, Hayley Berman, Derek Blackadder, Kirill Buketov, Roger Darlington, Stuart Derbyshire, Zoltan Dienes, Klaus-Dieter Rossade, Mark Felton, Pat Hews, Martin Lee, Alan Schamroth, and Martin S. Taylor.

In addition, I'd like to thank the staffs at the DSTL Secretariat (Porton Down), the London Library, The National Archives and the British Library.

And a very special thanks to Michael Leventhal, who came up with the idea.